Documents and Debates
General Editor: John Wroughton, M.A.,

Nineteenth Century Europe

Stephen Brooks

Research and Information Office,
Imperial War Museum

First published 1983
Reprinted 1984, 1985, 1987, 1990

Published by
MACMILLAN EDUCATION LTD
Houndmills, Basingstoke, Hampshire RG21 2XS
and London
Companies and representatives
throughout the world

Printed in Hong Kong

ISBN 0–333–28406–2

Contents

Acknowledgements

The author and publishers wish to thank the following who have kindly given permission for the use of copyright material:

George Allen & Unwin (Publishers) Ltd for an extract from *How the War Began in 1914* by B Schilling; Edward Arnold (Publishers) Ltd for an extract from *Documents of European Economic History II* by Sidney Pollard and Colin Holmes; Basil Blackwell Publishers Ltd for an extract from *Lectures on European History 1789–1914* by John McManners; Cambridge University Press for extracts from *The Cambridge History of British Foreign Policy 1783–1919* by Sir A. W. Ward and G. P. Gooch; *Ideology and Motivation in the Paris Commune of 1871* by R. D. Price, from *The Historical Journal* (1972), and *The Papers of Friedrich von Holstein*, Vol. II; Jonathan Cape Ltd on behalf of the Executors of the Serge Sazonov Estate for an extract from *Fateful Years 1909–16*; Librairie Armand Colin, Paris, for an extract from *The Triumph of the Middle Classes* by Charles Morazé; David & Charles Ltd for an extract from *Key Treaties of the Great Powers 1814–1914* Vol. I by Michael Hurst; Victor Gollancz Ltd for an extract from *A World Restored* by Henry Kissinger; Hamish Hamilton Ltd for an extract from *Vanished Supremacies: Essays on European History 1812–1918* by Sir Lewis Namier; Harper & Row Publishers Inc. for an extract from *France: Empire and Republic 1850–1940* by David Thomson; William Heinemann Ltd for an extract from *The Memoirs of Prince Chlodwig of Hohenlohe Schillingsfuerst*, translated by George W. Chrystal from the first German edition edited by Friedrich Curtius; Hodder & Stoughton Ltd for an extract from *The Second Empire* by Philip Guedalla; Alfred A. Knopf Inc. for an extract from *Europe Since Napoleon*, second edition, revised by David Thomson; Lawrence & Wishart Ltd for an extract from *Collected Works of Marx and Engels*, Vol. II (1979); Longman Group Ltd for extracts from the *Annual Register* 1820, 1848 and 1849; *From Bismark to Hitler* by J. C. G. Rohl and *British History in the Nineteenth Century and After* by G. M. Trevelyan; John Murray (Publishers) Ltd for an extract from *Bismark: The Man and the Statesman* Vol. II (1898); *The Observer* for an extract from a book review, 25 November 1979, by Theodore Zeldin; Oxford University Press for extracts from *Germany 1866–1945* by Gordon A. Craig (1978); *France 1848–1945* by Theodore Zeldin (1973); *Things I Remember* by Massimo d'Azeglio translated by E R Vincent (1966); *The Foundation of the German Empire: Selected Documents* by H Böhme (1971); *The History of My Contemporary* by V. G. Korolenko translated and abridged by Neil Parsons (1972); *Bonapartism* by H.A.L. Fisher (1908), and *The Origins of the War* by Luigi Albertini, Vols II and III (1953, 1957); Penguin Books Ltd for an extract from *Karl Marx: The First International and After* edited by David Fernbach (Pelican Marx Library/New Left Review, 1974); Prentice-Hall, Inc. Englewood Cliffs, NJ for an extract from 'The Monroe Doctrine' in *Documents of American History*, 5th edition, edited by Henry Steele Commager, © 1949; G. P. Putnam Ltd for an extract from *The Memoirs of Prince Von Bulow* Vol. IV translated by F. A. Voigt (1931) from the original German published by Verlag Ullstein; Sage Publications, London, for an extract from an article by Paul Kennedy published in *Journal of Contemporary History* January 1973; Dr Eugene Schulkind for an extract from his paper *The Paris Commune of 1871*, Historical Association Pamphlet G-78, 1971, published by The Historical Association; Maurice Temple Smith Ltd for an extract from *The Continental Commitment* by Michael Howard; The University of Chicago Press for an extract from *Journal of Modern History* (1948) by Hans Rothfels; University of Notre Dame Press for *Palacky: Letter to the German National Assembly* translated by Hans Kohn and reproduced in his book *Pan-Slavism, Its History and Ideology* (1953); Yale University Press for an extract from *A Source Book for Russian History from Early Times to 1917*, Vol. III, edited by George Vernadsky.

Every effort has been made to trace all the copyright holders but if any have been inadvertently overlooked the publishers will be pleased to make the necessary arrangements at the first opportunity.

The cover illustration is reproduced by kind permission of Hachette/Bibliothèque Nationale, Paris.

Europe in the Nineteenth Century

Over the past thirty years three main influences have affected our understanding and interpretation of European history in the nineteenth century. First, the scope of writing on the period, once dominated by political and diplomatic history, has widened to give greater emphasis to the discussion of economic, social and intellectual aspects of the life of the continent. In the preface to his book *A History of Italy 1700–1860*, Stuart Woolf makes a strong plea for yet more research to be done into the social history of nineteenth-century Italy in the following terms:

> I remain (indeed I have become ever more) convinced that political history, if it is to be more than just the recounting of a story, is so far from offering an autonomous approach that it can only be understood through the conditioning and slowly changing structures of society.

Secondly, in the more traditional areas of inquiry – the political, constitutional and diplomatic fields – new evidence continues to be found in public and private archives, whilst well-established sources are subjected to fresh scrutiny and key episodes examined in minute detail. Thirdly, as it becomes possible to take a more detached view of the cataclysmic events in the first half of the twentieth century, the significance of developments in Europe in the nineteenth century can be seen in a new perspective.

The effects of these three factors on the writing of nineteenth-century European history can be seen in a number of ways. Many long-accepted generalisations have fallen by the wayside, or at least been greatly modified. To give one instance, Louis Napoleon's failing health in the 1860s has traditionally been seen as contributing to the decline of the Second Empire, yet after looking closely at the evidence, Roger Williams, in his book *The Mortal Napoleon*, concludes that it 'fails to provide substantial proof for a single example of a political decision that would have been made differently had the emperor been free of arthritis, gout, hemorrhoids or the stone'. More broadly, the view which we now have of the pressures for continuity or change in any society has tended to modify our approach to the role of 'great men' in shaping the course of events. Finally, the creation of nation states in nineteenth-century Europe could no longer be regarded as a beneficial or 'natural' process once the excesses of nationalism had manifested themselves in the twentieth century and central Europe had been reshaped in the aftermath of the Second World War.

Nowhere has the impact of these changes been so great as in the study of German history. In 1961 Professor Barraclough wrote, 'There are probably few aspects of the traditional picture of nineteenth-century Europe more in need of reconsideration than the story of German unification'. This reappraisal is still taking place today. Studies have appeared on economic and social problems associated with the creation of a united Germany, generalisations about the growth of national consciousness have been re-examined and Bismarck's dominant role has been questioned. On this last point, Gordon A. Craig begins the opening chapter of his book *Germany 1866–1945* with a comment which forms an interesting counterweight to Stuart Woolf's statement quoted above:

> Is it a mistake to begin with Bismarck? So much is written these days, and so insistently, about the primary importance of economic and social forces in history that one runs the risk of being considered old-fashioned if one gives too much prominence to personality. Yet it is certainly unnecessary to apologise for introducing Bismarck's name at the outset. If he had never risen to the top in Prussian politics, the unification of Germany would probably have taken place anyway, but surely not at the same time or in quite the same way as it did. Whatever may be said about the movement of economic forces, there is no burking the fact that the decision concerning the form unification would take was made, not in the area of economic and commercial policy, but on the battlefield of Königrätz on 3 July 1866; and it would be idle to deny that when the broken fragments of Benedek's army retreated under the cover of their artillery to the banks of the Elbe on that dark afternoon, they were registering the triumph of Bismarck's policy.

Nineteenth-century Germany was the birthplace of modern 'scientific' historical scholarship, with the emphasis placed by Leopold von Ranke (1795–1886) at Berlin university on the primary importance of original records. It was Ranke who propounded the view that it was the historian's task to attempt to understand the past rather than to pass judgement on it – to try to show 'wie es eigentlich gewesen' ('how things really were'). Dr Paul Kennedy points out in his article 'The Decline of Nationalistic History in the West' (*Journal of Contemporary History*, January 1973), the paradox that it was Ranke's successors who produced the most blatantly nationalistic history as they came to act as propagandists for the policies of the new German empire. The historian Heinrich von Treitschke (1834–96) set out to educate the German people about the struggle for national unity, and his works form, in Kennedy's words, 'a paean of praise to the Prussian conservative state and to the unified Reich that Bismarck had established'.

It was in the face of this tradition of academic historical writing, which had naturally continued into the Nazi era, that in the 1960s the Hamburg historian, Fritz Fischer, produced his studies of German policy during and immediately before the First World War, which, in effect, placed the blame on Germany for the outbreak of the conflict (see section IX). This caused a furore amongst older German historians, at least one of whom accused Fischer of being a traitor to his country. The ensuing controversy expanded into a general debate on the continuity of the policies of Germany's leaders from 1870 to 1945 and on the question whether the roots of National Socialism can be detected in nineteenth-century Germany. Writing of Fischer in his book *From Bismarck to Hitler*, Dr J. C. G. Röhl says, 'Despite the initial outcry, his basic conclusions have now been widely accepted and his influence is clearly discernible in most of the monographs now appearing in Germany. Something of a historiographical revolution has occurred.'

History as national propaganda is now no longer acceptable in the west, but as Dr Kennedy says, 'Today's anti-nationalist historians exhibit some of the faults and weaknesses of their more chauvinist forebears. Types of prejudice may change: the existence of prejudice remains.' One of the themes of this book is the historian's need to be able to recognise bias of every kind in both primary and secondary sources. The sections have been chosen so that each one, as well as dealing with an important topic in nineteenth-century European history, also covers some general problems of historical study – the value of memoirs, the place of biography in historical writing, the influence of ideas on events and so on. No attempt has been made to include in a book of this size all of what might be thought of as the 'key' documents of nineteenth-century history – the Ems telegram and Germany's 'blank cheque' to Austria in 1914 have, for example, been omitted. One good reason for this is that such documents are conveniently available in G. A. Kertesz's *Documents in the Political History of the European Continent 1815–1939* (Oxford University Press, 1968), an indispensable companion to this volume. The relevant books in the *Problems in European Civilisation* series, published in the United States by D. C. Heath & Co., are also valuable for the greater scope they offer for the study of conflicts of interpretation between historians on particular issues. However, it must be recognised that no 'digests' can provide a test of one of the most important historical skills needed for the study of Europe in the nineteenth century – that is, the ability to 'see the wood for the trees' amongst the mass of primary and secondary sources which confront the historian on every issue.

The increasing volume and specialisation of research on nineteenth-century Europe has made it more and more difficult for any individual to keep fully up to date, for as Stuart Woolf says, 'New materials and new interpretations have continued to appear inexorably and sometimes with terrifying rapidity'. As Theodore Zeldin writes in his introduction to *France 1848–1945*, the result is that 'old generalisations survive tenaciously, even though the specialists have shown them to be false'. Even when new ideas are assimilated into general histories, they are 'usually fitted into a traditional framework somehow, rather than radically altering it'. It is nevertheless important to remember that detailed research and lengthy specialisation do not imply that the last word has been said on any subject, since the historical writing of today will itself be questioned by future generations of historians. In his conclusion to the second volume of *France 1848–1945*, Zeldin widens this point to make a thought-provoking justification for the study of history:

> Every generation is confused by its past and uncertain about the significance of its own times. The historian questions the generalisations that have become current about the past and its relations with the present. He tries to discover what people have been trying to do, which is not necessarily what they said or thought they were doing, and to show why plans went astray, why situations no one wanted came about. Historical study is a necessary preliminary to an understanding of the choices that each generation has to make, and to a reordering of the priorities it must have before it. The historian is not a soothsayer, he cannot tell what is going to happen next; but he may perhaps have some use all the same, in the sense that he can be a kind of court jester. He cultivates detachment. Humour, as has been shown, is one form of detachment. The historian tries to interest and entertain, but also to say what his readers may not wish to hear.

I Problems of Diplomacy, 1815–30

Introduction

The object of this first section is to examine the relations between the states of Europe in the aftermath of the Napoleonic wars. It also raises issues which can be used as the starting point for discussion of general problems involved in the study of international affairs in the nineteenth century. There are a number of interesting aspects to this period. First, we need to look at the problems of agreeing on a peace settlement and then keeping the peace after a long period when international disputes had been settled by force of arms. Secondly, there is the question of how the wartime alliance against France broke up when the threat from Napoleon ceased to unite its members. Thirdly, there is the problem of what was the real importance of the peacetime 'summit meetings' of the great powers, generally called the congress system. Fourthly, given that this period was one in which the diplomatic stage was occupied by a number of striking characters – Tsar Alexander, Metternich, Castlereagh and Canning – their personalities and qualities as statesmen provide fruitful topics for discussion.

The documents have been chosen to illustrate these themes. They also show various ways in which diplomats could communicate with – and try to influence – their opposite numbers in other states. The questions at the end of each extract provide opportunities to discuss how effective the methods were which this particular group of diplomats used. The section begins with the text of the Holy Alliance, the origins and importance of which have been the subject of much discussion between historians despite Castlereagh's description of it as a 'piece of sublime mysticism and nonsense'. This is followed by a selection of extracts which focus on the question of intervention by one state in the internal affairs of another, which David Thomson in document 6 describes as 'the fundamental issue of international relations'. The last document consists of two extracts from *A World Restored*, which Henry Kissinger wrote as a university professor before he himself became a diplomat. These extracts look at the peace settlement of 1815 and the period immediately following it in the context of nineteenth-century European history as a whole.

Nineteenth-century historians had little good to say for the Vienna peace-makers of 1814–15. They regarded them as 'mere hucksters in the diplomatic market bartering the happiness of millions with a scented smile', in Harold Nicolson's phrase. The blame for the fact that European rulers adopted reactionary policies after 1815 was laid at the door of Metternich, the 'high priest' of the Holy Alliance. In the twentieth century the peace-makers have had a better press from historians. The wisdom of their lenient treatment of France, and their difficulties in understanding how to deal with the new forces of liberalism and nationalism in Europe have been emphasised. Metternich's role as a 'cynical manipulator' and his influence on international relations have also been re-evaluated to present him in a more favourable light. Historians continue to debate the causes of the relative tranquillity of Europe for more than a generation after 1815. What emphasis should be given to the nature of the peace settlement itself? How much credit should the diplomats be given for their handling of the different crises which arose during the period? Or is the explanation that Europe's rulers, faced by the threat of disorder at home after a generation of war, simply lacked the confidence or resources to conduct adventurous foreign policies?

Further Reading

Three essential books are Frederick B. Artz, *Reaction and Revolution 1814–1832* (Harper, 1934), H. G. Schenk, *The Aftermath of the Napoleonic Wars* (Kegan Paul, 1947) and Henry A. Kissinger, *A World Restored* (Houghton Mifflin, 1957; Gollancz, 1973). A valuable recent collection of essays is Alan Sked (ed.), *Europe's Balance of Power 1815–48* (Macmillan, 1979). Harold Nicolson, *The Congress of Vienna* (Constable, 1946), covers the period 1812–22, as well as looking in detail at the negotiations at Vienna. For international relations after 1815 with the main focus on British policy, see Sir Charles Webster, *The Foreign Policy of Castlereagh*, vol II (Bell, 1925), Harold Temperley, *The Foreign Policy of Canning* (Bell, 1925) and R. W. Seton-Watson, *Britain in Europe* (Cambridge University Press, 1937). The way in which historians have differed regarding the interpretation of Metternich's role in international affairs is covered by the edited writings in a volume in the 'Problems in European Civilization' series: Henry F. Schwarz (ed.), *Metternich, the 'Coachman of Europe' – Statesman or Evil Genius?* (D. C. Heath & Co., 1962). M. S. Anderson, *The Eastern Question* (Macmillan, 1966), deals with the impact of the Greek revolt on international affairs in the 1820s. Memoirs and biographies of the leading statesmen of the period would be a valuable supplement to the works listed above: e.g. Alan Palmer, *Metternich: Councillor of Europe* (Weidenfeld & Nicolson, 1972) and John W. Derry, *Castlereagh* (Allen Lane, 1976).

1 The Holy Alliance, 26 September 1815

Their Majesties the Emperor of Austria, the King of Prussia, and the Emperor of Russia . . . solemnly declare that the present act has no other

object than to publish, in the face of the whole world, their fixed resolution, both in the administration of their respective states, and in
5 their political relations with every other government, to take for their sole guide the precepts of that Holy Religion; namely the precepts of justice, Christian charity and peace, which, far from being applicable only to private concerns, must have an immediate influence on the Councils of Princes, and guide all their steps, as being the only means of
10 consolidating human institutions, and remedying their imperfections . . . .

Conformably to the word of the Holy Scriptures, which command all men to consider each other as brethern, *the three contracting monarchs* will remain united by the bonds of a true and indissoluble fraternity, and
15 considering each other as fellow countrymen, they will on all occasions, and in all places, lend each other aid and assistance; *and regarding themselves towards their subjects and armies as fathers of families, they will lead them, in the same spirit of fraternity with which they are animated to protect religion, peace and justice. . . .*

20 All the Powers who shall choose solemnly to avow the sacred principles which have dictated the present act, and shall acknowledge how important it is for the happiness of nations, too long agitated, that these truths should henceforth exercise over the destinies of mankind all the influence which belongs to them, will be received with equal ardour
25 and affection into this holy alliance.

Michael Hurst (ed.), *Key Treaties of the Great Powers 1814–1914*, 1972, vol I, pp 96–7

Questions

a Metternich modified the original draft of the treaty which Tsar Alexander had drawn up by the following alterations:
(i) the words 'in future' were omitted after 'to take' (line 5);
(ii) the words 'as was hitherto believed' were omitted after 'private concerns' (line 8);
(iii) the words in italics (line 13) were substituted for 'the subjects of the three contracting parties';
(iv) the words in italics (lines 16–19) were substituted for 'the same will apply to the respective armies which will equally consider themselves as belonging only to the same army which is called upon to protect religion, peace and justice';
(v) the word 'Powers' was substituted for 'states' (line 20). What are the effects of these changes and why should Metternich have made them?

b What obligations did the signatories of the alliance undertake towards each other and towards their own subjects?

* *c* What motivated Alexander I in drawing up this strange-sounding document? Did its apparent idealism conceal more sinister designs?

* *d* Metternich's opinion on reading the tsar's original draft had been that it 'supplied no material for a treaty between Monarchs'. Why do you think he reacted in this way? Why did the emperor of Austria and the king of Prussia nevertheless agree to join the tsar in forming the alliance?
* *e* How did the other rulers of Europe respond to the invitation in the third paragraph of the extract? How far was Great Britain prepared to associate herself with the treaty?

2 The Issue of Intervention: Lord Castlereagh sets out the British viewpoint in a confidential State Paper circulated to the European governments, 5 May 1820

The events which have occurred in Spain have, as might be expected, excited . . . the utmost anxiety throughout Europe. . . . The British cabinet upon this, as upon all other occasions, is ever ready to deliberate with those of the Allies, and will unreservedly explain itself upon this 5 great question of common interest; but as to the form in which it may be prudent to conduct these deliberations, they conceive, they cannot too early recommend that course of deliberation which will excite the least attention or alarm, or which can least provoke jealousy in the minds of the Spanish nation or government. In this view, it appears to them 10 advisable, studiously to avoid any reunion of the Sovereigns; to abstain, at least in the present stage of the question, from charging any ostensible conference with commission to deliberate on the affairs of Spain. They conceive it preferable that their intercourse should be limited to those confidential communications between the cabinets, which are, in 15 themselves, best adapted to approximate ideas, and to lead, as far as may be, to the adoption of common principles, rather than to hazard a discussion in a ministerial conference, which, from the necessarily limited powers of the individuals composing it, must ever be better fitted to execute a purpose already decided upon, than to frame a course of policy 20 under delicate and difficult circumstances. . . .

The present state of Spain, no doubt, seriously extends the range of political agitation in Europe, but it must nevertheless be admitted, that there is no portion of Europe of equal magnitude, in which such a revolution could have happened, less likely to menace other states with 25 that direct and imminent danger, which has always been regarded, at least in this country, as alone constituting the case which would justify external interference. . . .

In this Alliance, as in all other human arrangements, nothing is more likely to impair, or even to destroy its real utility, than any attempt to 30 push its duties and its obligations beyond the sphere which its original conception and understood principles will warrant. It was an Union for

the re-conquest and liberation of a great proportion of the continent of Europe from the military dominion of France; and having subdued the conqueror, it took the state of possession, as established by the peace,
35 under the protection of the Alliance. It never was, however, intended as an Union for the government of the world, or for the superintendence of the internal affairs of other states. . . .

In Russia there is but little public sentiment with regard to Spain, which can embarrass the decision of the Sovereign; in Great Britain there
40 is a great deal, and the current of that sentiment runs strongly against the late policy of the King of Spain. Besides, the people of this country would probably not recognise (unless Portugal was attacked) that our safety could be so far menaced by any state of things in Spain, as to warrant their government in sending an army to that country to meddle in its internal
45 affairs. . . . In this country at all times, but especially at the present conjuncture, when the whole energy of the state is required to unite reasonable men in defence of our existing institutions, and to put down the spirit of treason and disaffection which in certain of the manufacturing districts in particular, pervades the lower orders, it is of the greatest
50 moment, that the public sentiment should not be distracted or divided, by any unnecessary interference of the governments in events, passing abroad, over which they can have none, or at best but very imperfect means of control. Nothing could be more injurious to the continental powers than to have their affairs made matter of daily discussion in our
55 Parliament, which nevertheless must be the consequence of their precipitately mixing themselves in the affairs of other states, if we should proceed *pari passu* with them in such interferences. . . . The fact is that we do not, and cannot feel alike upon all subjects. Our position, our institutions, the habits of thinking, and the prejudice of our people,
60 render us essentially different. . . .

There is at present very naturally a widespread apprehension of the fatal consequences to the public tranquillity of Europe, that may be expected to flow from the dangerous principles of the present day, at work more or less in every European state. [But given the military
65 weakness of Spain and France, if the other states of Europe] can preserve harmony among themselves, and exercise a proper degree of vigilance with respect to their interior police, there is nothing in this state of things which should prevent them from abiding with patience and with firmness the result of the great political process to which circumstances
70 have given existence in the states to the westward of their frontiers. . . .

We shall be found in our place when actual danger menaces the system of Europe; but this country cannot, and will not, act upon abstract and speculative principles of precaution. The Alliance which exists had no such purpose in view in its original formation. It was never so explained
75 to Parliament; if it had, most assuredly the sanction of Parliament would never have been given to it.

Sir A. W. Ward and G. P. Gooch (eds), *The Cambridge History of British Foreign Policy 1783–1919*, 1923, vol II, pp 623–32

Questions

a What is meant by the following in this extract: (i) 'The events which have occurred in Spain' (line 1); (ii) '*pari passu*' (line 57)?

b Paraphrase the following sentences: lines 12–20; 28–31; 64–70; 71–3.

c To which treaties is Castlereagh referring when he uses the terms 'Alliance' and 'Union'? How does he define the limitations on the 'duties' and 'obligations' (line 30) which Britain accepted when she joined the alliance, and why does he believe that the events in Spain fall outside the scope of these obligations?

d Castlereagh believes that it is not the correct time for a full-scale congress or ministerial meeting to deliberate on events in Spain. What arguments does he use to support his case and what reasons might he have omitted from a document intended for circulation to the other governments of Europe?

* *e* How did the nature of British society and government affect Castlereagh's formulation of his policy on Spain? Why was Britain 'essentially different' (line 60) from the continental powers in her response to revolts on the mainland of Europe?

f In what ways does Castlereagh take advantage of the fact that this is a *confidential* memorandum by putting forward arguments which he could not have used in a public document?

3 The Issue of Intervention: the Holy Alliance's View, from a Circular Note of the Courts of Austria, Russia and Prussia to the Ministers and Chargés d'Affaires at the German and Northern Courts, 8 December 1820

Informed of the false and extravagant reports respecting the object and the results of the conference at Troppau, which malevolent persons have put into circulation and the credulous have further disseminated, the allied courts consider it to be necessary to give authentic explanations to
5 their ministers at foreign courts, to enable them to correct the mistakes and false opinions occasioned by these reports. . . .

The events of the 8th March, in Spain; of 2nd July, in Naples; and the catastrophe of Portugal could not but excite a deep feeling of uneasiness and sorrow in all those who are bound to provide for the security of states,
10 and at the same time to inspire them with a desire to unite and jointly to take into consideration how to eradicate all the evils which threatened to break out over Europe. It was natural that these feelings should especially influence those powers who had lately conquered the revolution, and now see it raise its head anew; and it was equally natural that those

15 Powers, in order to oppose it for the third time, should have recourse to the same means of which they had made so successful a use in the memorable contest which freed Europe from a yoke it had borne for twenty years . . . .

The Powers exercised an undisputed right, when they considered of 20 joint measures of precautions against states, in which an overthrow of the Government, effected by rebellion, even considered only as an example, must give rise to a hostile attitude. Towards all legitimate constitutions and governments the exercise of this right became the more urgent when those who had come into this situation endeavoured to communicate the 25 misfortune which they had drawn on themselves to the neighbouring countries. . . .

The system adopted between Austria, Russia and Prussia is not a new one; it reposes on the same maxims which were the basis of the treaties by which the Union of European States was founded. The intimate 30 harmony between the courts which are in the centre of this union can only gain by it in strength and duration. The Union will consolidate itself in the same manner as it was formed by the Monarchs who founded it, and has been gradually adopted by all those who were convinced of its evident, now less then ever to be doubted, advantages. No further proof 35 is necessary, that neither thoughts of conquest, nor the pretensions to violate the independence of other governments in their internal administration, nor the endeavour to impede voluntary and wise ameliorations, consonant with the true interest of nations, has had any share in the resolutions of the Allied Powers.

Annual Register 1820, pp 735–7

Questions

a Give the meaning of the following words: 'credulous' (line 3); 'maxims' (line 28); 'ameliorations' (line 38).

b What is the purpose of the Circular Note? What can you deduce from it about the nature of the 'false and extravagant reports' (line 1) regarding the congress of Troppau, and how does it rebut these criticisms?

c In what respects were Austria, Prussia and Russia attempting to learn from the mistakes of their policies towards revolutionary and Napoleonic France? How would Castlereagh have argued that circumstances were different in 1820?

d What is the significance of the phrase 'consonant with the true interest of nations' (line 38)?

* *e* Is there any evidence that the revolts of 1820 were co-ordinated or connected which would justify the claim that the revolutionaries were endeavouring 'to communicate the misfortune . . . countries' (lines 24–6)?

4 The Issue of Intervention: Metternich's view of revolutions expressed in a secret memorandum to Tsar Alexander, 15 December 1820

Kings have to calculate the chances of their very existence in the immediate future; passions are let loose, and league together to overthrow everything which society respects as the basis of its existence; religion, public morality, laws, customs, rights, and duties, all are
5 attacked, confounded, overthrown, or called into question. The great mass of the people are tranquil spectators of these attacks and revolutions, and of the absolute want of all means of defence. A few are carried off by the torrent, but the wishes of the immense majority are to maintain a repose which exists no longer, and of which even the first elements seem
10 to be lost. . . . We are convinced that society can no longer be saved without strong and vigorous resolutions on the part of the Governments still free in their opinions and actions. . . . The first principle to be followed by the monarchs, united as they are by the coincidence of their desires and opinions, should be that of maintaining the stability of
15 political institutions against the disorganised excitement which has taken possession of men's minds; the immutability of principles against the madness of their interpretation; and respect for laws actually in force against a desire for their destruction. . . . In short, let the great monarchs strengthen their union, and prove to the world that if it exists, it is
20 beneficent, and ensures the political peace of Europe; that it is powerful only for the maintenance of tranquillity at a time when so many attacks are directed against it; that the principles which they profess are paternal and protective, menacing only disturbers of public tranquillity.

Memoirs of Prince Metternich, 1881, vol III, pp 454 ff

Questions

a Give the meaning of the following words: 'immutability' (line 16); 'beneficent' (line 20); 'paternal' (line 22).

* *b* What were the 'passions' (line 2) which were disturbing Europe in 1820?

c What was Metternich's object in sending what he termed this 'Confession of Faith' to the tsar in December 1820? How is its style and content designed to have the most influence on Alexander?

* *d* Metternich regarded himself as the 'doctor of revolutions'. What are his diagnosis and prescription expressed here regarding the events of 1820? Was his analysis correct?

* *e* To what extent were Austria, Prussia and Russia united 'by the coincidence of their desires and opinions' (lines 13–4) in the period 1815–30?

* *f* What principles guided Metternich's formulation of Austrian foreign policy up to 1848?

5 The Issue of Intervention: President Monroe expresses the United States' view in his annual message to Congress, 2 December 1823

We owe it, therefore, to candour and to the amicable relations existing between the United States and those European powers to declare that we should consider any attempt on their part to extend their system to any portion of this hemisphere as dangerous to our peace and safety. . . .

5 The late events in Spain and Portugal show that Europe is still unsettled. Of this important fact no stronger proof can be adduced than that the allied powers should have thought it proper, on any principle satisfactory to themselves, to have interposed by force in the internal concerns of Spain. To what extent such interposition may be carried, on

10 the same principle, is a question in which all independent powers whose governments differ from theirs are interested, even those most remote, and surely none more so than the United States. Our policy in regard to Europe, which was adopted at an early stage of the wars which have so long agitated that quarter of the globe, nevertheless remains the same,

15 which is, not to interfere in the internal concerns of any of its powers; to consider the government *de facto* as the legitimate government for us; to cultivate friendly relations with it, and to preserve those relations by a frank, firm, and manly policy, meeting in all instances the just claims of every power, submitting to injuries from none. But in regard to these

20 continents circumstances are eminently and conspicuously different. It is impossible that the allied powers should extend their political system to any portion of either continent without endangering our peace and happiness; nor can anyone believe that our southern brethren, if left to themselves, would adopt it of their own accord. It is equally impossible,

25 therefore, that we should behold such interposition in any form with indifference. If we look to the comparative strength and resources of Spain and those new Governments, and their distance from each other, it must be obvious that she can never subdue them. It is still the true policy of the United States to leave the parties to themselves, in the hope that

30 other powers will pursue the same course.

Henry Steele Commager (ed.), *Documents of American History*, 1949, pp 236–7

Questions

a What is meant by the following in the above extract: (i) the wars . . . globe' (lines 13–14); (ii) 'to consider . . . for us' (lines 15–16); (iii) 'our southern brethren' (line 23)?

* *b* When was James Monroe president of the United States? Which party did he represent?

* *c* Comment on the timing of President Monroe's statement in relation to events in Europe and to the possibility of European involvement on the American continent.

* *d* Why was the issue of the future of former colonies in South America of great importance to Britain? How did it contribute to Britain's breach with her former allies in Europe?

e How far were the principles of the Monroe Doctrine observed in the relations between Europe and the American continent up to 1914?

* *f* What episodes in the relations between Europe and the United States in the twentieth century strike parallels with the attitudes expressed here by President Monroe?

6 The Issue of Intervention: an Historian's View

In so far as the congress system meant that the great powers of Europe could usefully meet together from time to time to resolve disputes among them and to preserve a certain balance of power in the continent, it met with partial success and helped to keep the peace. At successive congresses
5 such questions as the abolition of slavery, navigation of the Danube, and arbitration of disputes were considered. But in so far as it came to serve the purposes of the Holy Alliance and of at least some of the partners of the Quadruple Alliance, it was a disturbing force in Europe. The principle of joint intervention, generally accepted in reference to the ex-enemy
10 state of France, became an excuse for a universal meddlesomeness that chimed with the real interests neither of Metternich nor of Britain. Each power in turn was prompted to intervene: Austria in Piedmont and Naples, France in Spain and Greece, Britain in Portugal and Greece, Russia in Greece. Britain, alarmed by the interventions of reactionary
15 monarchs and by the ambiguous aims of Russia in Turkey, found herself committed to the paradoxical policy of 'intervening to prevent intervention'. Even the long and tense achievement of 'holding the ring' during the Greek revolution broke down in the end, and meanwhile brought terrible losses to the Greeks. The protest of the Monroe
20 Doctrine against the practice of intervention for or against existing regimes helped to force upon public attention the fundamental issue of international relations. Neither the forces of conservatism nor those of nationalism and liberalism derived unmitigated benefits from it. Intervention favoured monarchs in Spain and Naples, liberal rebels in
25 Portugal and Greece; but neither dynastic monarchy nor national independence stood to gain in the long run from accepting the doctrine that external powers might properly intervene in the internal affairs of states. It was discovered by experience that the congress system could mean generalizing, and so magnifying, every dispute; it meant alerting
30 governments everywhere whenever there was an insurrection anywhere. By making peace 'indivisible' it made peace more fragile, for the rival interests of the major powers were implicated in each revolutionary crisis. The 'concert of Europe', viewed by the conservative powers as a dam against revolution, was thought of by Britain rather as a sluice gate,

35 allowing for a measured flow of national and liberal progress. This conflict of purposes was to last for half a century.

David Thomson, *Europe Since Napoleon*, 1977, pp 139–40

Questions

a What do you understand by the terms: (i) 'balance of power' (line 3); (ii) 'concert of Europe' (line 33)?

b What does David Thomson see as the valuable aspects of the congresss system?

c Why does David Thomson ultimately regard the congress system as a 'disturbing force in Europe' (line 8)?

* *d* David Thomson expresses the view that the 'principle of joint intervention' was not in the 'real interests' of either Britain or Austria. Do you agree? What do you think the 'real interests' of Britain and Austria were at this period?

* *e* Discuss Canning's statement that 'conferences are useless or dangerous – useless if we are in agreement, dangerous if we are not', in the light of events in Europe 1818–25 and the above extract.

7 An Historian and Diplomat reflects on the Congress Era

(a) When Napoleon was defeated in Russia, the problem of constructing a legitimate order confronted Europe in its most concrete form. For opposition can create a wide consensus, perhaps even the widest attainable one, but its components, united by what they do not like, may
5 be greatly at odds about what should replace it. It is for this reason that the year 1812 is the starting point of our discussion. However one conceives it – and it has been given a variety of interpretations ranging from the moral vindication of national self-determination to the tragic destiny of the Hero – this year marked the moment when it became evident that
10 Europe was not to be organised by force. But the alternative was not nearly so apparent. It was clear that there were new forces loose in the world clamouring for popular participation in government. But it seemed equally evident that these forces had been responsible for a quarter-century of turmoil. The French Revolution had dealt a perhaps
15 mortal blow to the divine right of Kings; yet the representatives of this very doctrine were called upon to end the generation of bloodshed. In these circumstances what is surprising is not how imperfect was the settlement that emerged, but how sane; not how 'reactionary' according to the self-righteous doctrines of nineteenth-century historiography, but
20 how balanced. It may not have fulfilled all the hopes of an idealistic generation, but it gave this generation something perhaps more precious: a period of stability which permitted their hopes to be realized without a major war or a permanent revolution. And our account will end in 1822,

when the international order which emerged out of the revolutionary
25 conflict assumed the form it was to retain for over a generation. The period of stability which ensued was the best proof that a 'legitimate' order had been constructed, an order accepted by all the major powers, so that henceforth they sought adjustment within its framework rather than in its overthrow. . . .

30 (b) . . . the intervention in Spain caused Great Britain to break openly with the Alliance. So ended Castlereagh's vision of a Europe united by the self-evident requirements of harmony. But it had lasted long enough to enable the European order to be taken for granted, the most difficult step in achieving permanence. Perhaps never again has European unity been
35 so much a reality as between 1815 and 1821, so much so that it came to be forgotten with what forebodings the Vienna settlement had been greeted by Gentz, who predicted a major war within five years, and by Castlereagh himself, who thought it would do well if it prevented another conflict for a decade. Not for a century was Europe to know a
40 major war, however, because in the interval the myth of a united Europe had been reduced to political terms, which enabled Metternich first to dominate Europe morally and then to construct a grouping of powers which made a major conflict impossible physically. By the time Britain withdrew from the Alliance, the elements of the equilibrium had been
45 established: the legitimising principle defined at Laibach served as the bond for the three Eastern powers, Prussia, Russia and Austria, which confronted a France unable to conduct a Continental policy against their united opposition and Britain increasingly aware of its extra-European role. Because the moral frame work of the Eastern bloc was defined by
50 Austria, the policy of the dominant group of powers was conservative and status quo and did not for this reason lead to the active hostility of Great Britain. To be sure, for a brief interval after the death of Alexander, Russia pursued an independent policy in the Balkans, allied with Great Britain. But the revolutions in Western Europe in 1830 served to
55 demonstrate to the new Tsar the correctness of Metternich's maxims of the danger of social upheaval, and the constellation of powers remained for over a generation with the 'Holy Alliance' predominant on the Continent and Great Britain across the seas.

Henry Kissinger, *A World Restored*, 1957, pp 4–5, 315

Questions

a What is meant by the following: (i) 'For opposition . . . replace it.' (lines 2–5); (ii) 'It was clear that . . . turmoil.' (lines 11–14); (iii) 'the divine right of Kings' (line 15); (iv) 'historiography' (line 19); (v) 'So ended . . . harmony.' (lines 31–2); (vi) 'Because the moral . . . Great Britain.' (lines 49–52)?

b What reasons does Kissinger give for taking 1812 as the starting point and 1822 as the end of his study?

* *c* Why should Kissinger have formulated a different view of the peace settlement from that of the nineteenth-century historians he criticises? Do you think Kissinger's view is too favourable?

* *d* Comment on Kissinger's assertion that there were no major wars in nineteenth-century Europe (lines 39–40).

e In the light of these extracts what principles do you think guided Henry Kissinger in his attempts to solve the problems of the Middle East and Vietnam by diplomatic means in the 1970s? Can politicians learn from the experience of the past?

f Do you see these extracts as reflecting more the attitude of an historian or a practical politician and diplomat?

Further Work

a 'Europe's relative tranquillity in the period 1815 to 1854 was more in spite of than because of the peace settlement of 1815.' Do you agree?

b Should the congress system be regarded as a failure?

c Why do diplomats sometimes choose to conduct their business with other countries in private and sometimes in public? Illustrate your answer with examples from the extracts in this section. Why is it important to know by whom a document was intended to be read before assessing its value as historical evidence?

II Risorgimento and Unification: Italy, 1815–70

Introduction

For many years historians tended to regard the unification of Italy as a subject for eulogy rather than critical scrutiny. For the Italian historian Benedetto Croce, writing in 1933, Italy's progress towards unity and independence was 'accompanied by the sympathy, the anxiety and the admiration of the whole world' and its eventual achievement was 'the masterpiece of the liberal–national movements of the nineteenth century'. The dramatic events of 1859–61 were seen as the climax of a national revival, the Risorgimento, dating back before the Napoleonic period to the eighteenth century. In fact, the influence of ideas on events is always a difficult subject for the historian and, as Derek Beales says, 'the precise relationship between the Risorgimento and the unification of Italy is exceedingly hard to determine'.

Since the Second World War historians have adopted a somewhat more critical approach to the 'romantic drama' of Italian unification, and Stuart Woolf writes of this as having led to a 'radical and deep revision of the traditional interpretation of the Risorgimento as the triumphantly inevitable culmination of the previous history of Italy'. First, the idea that from an early stage nationalist ideals, inspired by the Risorgimento, motivated Italian nationalists has been questioned. For instance, whilst acknowledging the importance of the lessons and legends of the upheavals of 1848–9, Agatha Ramm believes that there was 'no singleness of purpose, no clearness or largeness of aim, to justify our considering the uprisings of 1848–49 truly nationalist'.

Secondly, the picture of Cavour as the 'master-builder' of Italian unity has been re-assessed, mainly in the writings of Denis Mack Smith. He concludes that Cavour did not have the firm grip on the situation in 1859–61 that the 'heroic' version of the story suggested, and that his relationship with Garibaldi was 'sometimes treacherous, often uncertain, and always more or less hostile'. Mazzini's role has also been reconsidered. The extent of his influence at different levels of Italian society has been questioned and Marxist historians in Italy, such as Antonio Gramsci, have criticised him for failing to develop a programme of agrarian reform which would have roused the peasantry in his support. Opponents of this view assert that any attempt at a social revolution would have ended in disaster and halted progress on unification, whereas Mazzini in fact provided the essential spur even after the failures of 1848–9. The interplay of forces and personalities is assessed by Stuart Woolf in the final extract in this section.

The documents in this section include words written by Mazzini in 1831 and 1871, from the idealism of his youth to the disillusionment of his old age. Recent historians have given a good deal of attention to the important question of whether the circumstances in which Italy gained her independence and unification damaged the prospects of the new state. This debate centres on the idea that the Risorgimento was 'une révolution manquée', a movement which neglected vital social and economic problems and 'eliminated the masses from participation in politics'. Mazzini himself had no doubts in 1871: 'The Italy which we represent today, like it or not, is a living lie.'

Further Reading

There are three excellent collections of documents with introductions on the unification of Italy: Denis Mack Smith (ed.), *The Making of Italy 1796–1866* (Macmillan, 1968), Stuart Woolf, *The Italian Risorgimento* (Longman, 1969) and Derek Beales, *The Risorgimento and the Unification of Italy* (Allen & Unwin 1971). There are two useful Historical Association pamphlets: Agatha Ramm, *The Risorgimento* (pamphlet 50, 1962), which surveys the points on which historians have disagreed about the subject, and H. Hearder, *Cavour* (pamphlet 80, 1972). There is a thought-provoking essay on 'Cavour and Garibaldi' in A. J. P. Taylor, *Europe: Grandeur and Decline* (Pelican, 1967), which is, in fact, a review of Denis Mack Smith, *Cavour and Garibaldi 1860* (Cambridge University Press, 1954). See also Denis Mack Smith, *Victor Emmanuel, Cavour and the Risorgimento* (Oxford University Press, 1971), Edgar Holt, *Risorgimento: the Making of Italy 1815–70* (Macmillan, 1970) and most recently Stuart Woolf, *A History of Italy 1700–1860* (Methuen, 1979). This last book is particularly valuable for the economic and social history of nineteenth-century Italy.

1 Mazzini's Instructions to Members of his Young Italy Movement, 1831

Young Italy is a brotherhood of Italians who believe in a law of progress and duty, and are convinced that Italy is destined to become one nation, convinced also that she possesses sufficient strength within herself to become one, and that the ill success of her former efforts is to be attributed
5 not to weakness, but to the misdirection of the revolutionary elements within her, – that the secret force lies in constancy and unity of effort. They join this association with the firm intention of consecrating both thought and action to the great aim of reconstituting Italy as one independent sovereign nation of free men and equals. . .
10 The aim of the association is revolution; but its labours will be

essentially educational, both before and after the day of revolution; and it therefore declares the principles upon which the national education should be conducted, and from which alone Italy may hope for safety and regeneration. . . .

15 Young Italy is republican and unitarian – republican, because theoretically every nation is destined, by the law of God and humanity, to form a free and equal community of brothers; and the republican form of government is the only form of government that insures this future: all true sovereignty resides essentially in the nation, the sole progressive and 20 continuous interpreter of the supreme moral law; . . . because the inevitable tendency of the series of progressive transformations taking place in Europe is toward the enthronement of the republican principle, and because the inauguration of the monarchical principle in Italy would carry along with it the necessity of a new revolution shortly after. . . .

25 Young Italy is unitarian, because, without unity there is no true nation; because, without unity there is no real strength; and Italy, surrounded as she is by powerful, united, and jealous nations, has need of strength above all things; because federalism, by reducing her to the political impotence of Switzerland, would necessarily place her under the influence of one of 30 the neighbouring nations; because federalism, by reviving the local rivalries now extinct, would throw Italy back upon the Middle Ages; . . . because federalism, by destroying the unity of the great Italian family, would strike at the root of the great mission Italy is destined to accomplish for humanity; because Europe is undergoing a progressive 35 series of transformations, which are gradually and irresistibly guiding European society to form itself into vast and united masses; because the entire work of internal civilisation in Italy will be seen, if rightly studied, to have been tending for ages toward unity.

The means by which Young Italy proposes to reach its aim are 40 education and insurrection, to be adopted simultaneously and made to harmonise with each other. Education must ever be directed to teach, by example, word, and pen, the necessity of insurrection. Insurrection, whenever it can be realised, must be so conducted as to render it a means of national education.

Milton Viorst (ed.), *The Great Documents of Western Civilisation*, 1965, pp 274–5

Questions

* *a* Who was Giuseppe Mazzini? What events and ideas produced a man like Mazzini at this stage in Italian history?

b What kind of Italy does the Young Italy movement wish to create? Why are alternative forms rejected?

c How are the aims of the movement to be achieved? What does Mazzini believe to be the value of revolts?

d How sound is Mazzini's interpretation of the trend of Italian history before 1831?

* *e* What forces in Italy before 1848 were working for and against national unity? How far did the Young Italy movement help or hinder the process of unification?

2 Massimo d'Azeglio reports to Charles Albert, King of Piedmont, in October 1845 on his visit to Central Italy

As was Charles Albert's practice, the audience took place at six o'clock in the morning. . . . At that time the king was a mystery; and although his later conduct has been plainly intelligible, he will perhaps remain partly a mystery, even for history. . . .

5 'Your Majesty is not ignorant of all unrest, plots, and little revolutions which have occurred since 1814. . . . The uselessness, indeed the harm, of such activities, which only serve to denude the country of its best men and exacerbate the foreign influence, has now struck the more intelligent people in Italy, and they want to discover a new path to take. . . .I

10 think I can assure you, without fear of deceiving myself, that the majority of them recognise the absurdity of what has hitherto happened and want to change their policy. All are persuaded that without force nothing can be done; that the only force in Italy is that of Piedmont; but that they cannot count even on this as long as Europe is peaceful and

15 organised as at present. These ideas are sensible and give proof of a real advance in political understanding. . . . This is why I have tried to restrain a new outbreak of desperation with a new idea, and for this purpose I have gone about to spread it, as I have reported. I think, despite the case of Rimini, my efforts have borne some fruit. Perhaps Your

20 Majesty will tell me if he approves, or not, of what I have done and what I have now said.'

I stopped and awaited the reply, which, to judge by the King's expression, did not seem likely to be hostile. But I guessed that, in regard to the essential, it was likely to be sibylline, and that it would not leave

25 one any the wiser. Instead, he said quietly but firmly, without any hesitation or turning his glance away, but looking me straight in the eyes: 'Let those gentlemen know that they should remain quiet and take no steps now, as nothing can be done at present; but they can rest assured that when the opportunity arises, my life, my children's lives, my arms, my

30 treasure, my army, all shall be given in the cause of Italy.'

Expecting something quite different, I remained for a moment speechless. . . . The intentions he had so resolutely revealed to me, especially the phrase 'Let those gentlemen know', had so surprised me that they did not yet seem real. . . . He nodded to show I had understood

35 him, and then dismissed me. We both got up; he placed his hands on my shoulders, and offered me his cheek, first on one side, then on the other.

However, this embrace seemed somewhat studied, cold, almost funereal, so that I felt chilled. An inner voice repeated that terrible phrase: 'Don't trust him.' It is a tremendous punishment for those who are professedly
40 astute, to be suspected, even when telling the truth. He had really spoken the truth, poor gentleman: events proved it. . . .

I returned to my little room on the top floor of the Trombetta Hotel, and sat down at the desk to write at once to my correspondents, who had to pass on the reply to all the others. . . . [My letter] gave the exact
45 purport of Charles Albert's reply; but to be scrupulously exact and in order not to give as certain what was really my own impression, I ended my letter: 'These are his words: God alone knows his inner thoughts.'

Massimo d'Azeglio, *Things I Remember*, from an English translation by E. R. Vincent, 1966 (this episode having been omitted from the first version of d' Azeglio's memoirs in 1868), pp 338–42

Questions

* *a* Who was Massimo d'Azeglio?

b What is meant by the following: (i) 'the case of Rimini' (line 19); (ii) 'it was likely to be sibylline' (line 24)?

c What is Massimo d'Azeglio's 'new idea' (line 17)?

* *d* What effect, according to d'Azeglio, have the activities inspired by the Young Italy movement had on attitudes to the unification of Italy? Is his opinion expressed in these circumstances a reliable one?

* *e* Why did Massimo d'Azeglio regard Charles Albert with such suspicion? Why was he particularly surprised by the phrase 'Let those gentlemen know' (line 33)?

* *f* In the light of Charles Albert's actions in 1848–9, should this extract be taken as proof that he was a genuine Italian patriot?

3 Allocution of Pope Pius IX delivered on 29 April 1848

We at the outset, not stimulated by encouragements or advice, but prompted by our own singular affection towards the people placed under the temporal dominion of the Church, granted more large indulgence to those who had departed from their duty of allegiance to
5 the pontifical government; and We subsequently made speed to adopt certain measures, which We had judged conducive in themselves to the prosperity of that people. And the whole of the acts which We have thus performed at the very commencement of our Pontificate are in thorough correspondence with those most anxious desires of the
10 European sovereigns.

But when, by the help of God, our plans had been brought to practical effect, not only our own people but those of neighbouring

states manifested an exulting joy, and applauded Us with public congratulations and testimonials of respect, in such a mode as made it our
15 duty to take care, even in this exalted City, to keep within due bounds popular outbursts, acclamations, and assemblages, that broke forth with an excess of vehemence. . . .

Seeing that some at present desire that We too, along with the other princes of Italy and their subjects, should engage in war against the
20 Austrians, We have thought it convenient to proclaim clearly and openly, in this our solemn assembly, that such a measure is altogether alien from our counsels, inasmuch as We, albeit unworthy, are upon earth the vice-gerent of Him that is the Author of Peace and the Lover of Charity, and, conformably to the function of our supreme apostolate,
25 We reach to and embrace all kindreds, peoples, and nations, with equal solicitude of paternal affection. But if, notwithstanding, there are not wanting among our subjects those who allow themselves to be carried away by the example of the rest of the Italians, in what manner could We possibly curb their ardour?

30 And in this place We cannot refrain from repudiating, before the face of all nations, the treacherous advice, published moreover in journals, and in various works, of those who would have the Roman Pontiff to be the head and to preside over the formation of some sort of novel republic of the whole Italian people. Rather, on this occasion, moved hereto by the
35 love We bear them, We do urgently warn and exhort the said Italian people to abstain with all diligence from the like counsels, deceitful and ruinous to Italy herself, and to abide in close attachment to their respective sovereigns, of whose good will they have already had experience, so as never to let themselves be torn away from the obedience
40 they owe them.

L. C. Farini, *The Roman State from 1815 to 1850*, 1851, vol II, pp. 106–11

Questions

* *a* What was the situation in Italy at the end of April 1848 when Pius IX made this statement?

* *b* What were the 'certain measures' (line 6) which Pius had adopted? In what way had 'the European sovereigns' been concerned with the affairs of the papacy before his election?

* *c* Why does Pius IX reject the idea of papal involvement in the war against Austria? Could his earlier actions have misled Italian nationalists about the role he might play?

d How would you interpret the sentence 'But if . . . their ardour?' (lines 26–9)

* *e* What is the plan for Italian unification which Pius repudiates in this document? Why was it called the 'Neo-Guelph' solution? Mention one writer who advocated it.

* *f* In what ways did the position of the papacy and those who wrote about it help or hinder progress towards unification 1815–49?

4 Cavour writes to Napoleon III, 19 March 1859

Your Majesty knows the difficulty of our position. We concerted a plan with Your Majesty by which we would group around us all the live forces of Italy, but without allowing our cause to be contaminated by any revolutionary element. For this we need the help of a great moral force, 5 such for instance as largely came to us from the support of Your Majesty and the weight which this gave us in Europe. But if we now are made to wait outside the door while others discuss the fate of Italy, in a Congress moreover where Your Majesty plays the chief role, the rest of Italy will see us as feeble and powerless. Even in Piedmont, opposition will grow, 10 and it will be hard to go on governing without exceptional measures and the use of force.

I beg Your Majesty to take into account what I here frankly put before you. I am not moved by any puerile vanity or by exaggerated notion of our importance, it is just that our exclusion from a Congress would 15 deprive us of the strength and prestige which we need for that great enterprise which is our duty and our right and which would for ever be the glory of your reign. Incidentally, I think that if you support us by formally asking for Piedmont's admission to the Congress, Austria will have to refuse, and we will then escape from this great danger.

20 If, on the other hand, Austria does agree to debate the Italian Question with us, I think we ought to have the agenda quite clear first. Vienna does not intend to make serious concessions: for instance she will not give up her protectorate over the Duchies, nor over Tuscany and the papal Legations; so that she will probably refuse to agree to this preliminary 25 request, in which case it will be her responsibility if the Congress does not take place.

I flatter myself that Your Majesty will know how to frustrate all the attempts of your enemies to prevent you accomplishing the noblest of all tasks. Your wisdom, your prudence, your moderation, and the loftiness 30 of your ideas, will together recover the support of public opinion which may have momentarily wavered. Austria has misjudged you and adopted a menacing or even provocative tone. She is playing the role of aggressor. And this makes me hope that before long she will commit one of those aggressive acts which will justify your armed intervention. I hope so with 35 all my heart.

Denis Mack Smith (ed.), *The Making of Italy 1796–1866*, 1968, p 272

Questions

a Explain the sentence 'We concerted a plan . . . element.' (lines 1–4).

b Explain the reference to a 'Congress' (line 7). What dangers does Cavour see in such a congress?

c In writing to Costantino Nigra on the same day, Cavour said of this letter, 'I avoided threats and declamations, but I tried to be as positive as possible.' What are the positive steps Cavour suggests to Napoleon III? What ploys does he use to sway the emperor?

d How had Cavour increased Piedmont's 'strength and prestige' (line 15) during the 1850s? Why did he now believe this to be at risk?

* *e* 'She is playing the role of aggressor' (line 32). Comment on Cavour's statement regarding Austria.

* *f* To what extent did Napoleon III's intervention in Italian affairs in 1859 go according to plan as far as Cavour was concerned?

5 The Secretary of the French Embassy in Turin, Henri d'Ideville, records in his journal in 1861 his opinion of King Victor Emmanuel

The immense popularity he enjoys in the old provinces of Piedmont owes more to the monarchical sentiments of the people than to the personal qualities of the King . . . . Events, and above all the genius of his Prime Minister, have raised him to the position he now occupies in Italy and
5 Europe. If ever his name becomes famous in history, his only glory will have been 'to have allowed Italy to create herself' . . . .

Like all mediocre men, Victor Emmanuel is jealous and quick to take umbrage. He will find it difficult to forget the manner of his triumphal entry into Naples, when, seated in Garibaldi's carriage – Garibaldi in a
10 red shirt – he was presented to his new people by the most powerful of all his subjects. People are mistaken in crediting Victor Emmanuel with a lively liking for Garibaldi. As soldiers they probably have points of contact in their characters and tastes, which have allowed them at times to understand each other and join forces; but the hero's republican, often
15 protective, familiarity is very displeasing to the descendant of the House of Savoy. After all, what sovereign, placed in the same situation, would not resent the fabulous prestige of Garibaldi's name? In any case, the frankness with which the King has spoken of him on certain occasions shows the real measure of his appreciation of the man. It was in the month
20 of June 1860; Garibaldi had just landed in Sicily, and the result of his venturesome expedition was not yet known in Turin, when the French minister, Baron de Talleyrand, was ordered to present a note to the Turin cabinet in which the Emperor's government, while complaining bitterly of this fresh violation of the Law of Nations, referred to the fact that they
25 were fully aware of the understanding between the Sardinian cabinet and Garibaldi. After a frank discussion with the Comte de Cavour, M. de Talleyrand asked to see the King. After his audience with the sovereign, the French minister felt convinced that His Majesty was far less pleased

with the hero's attempt than people imagined. '*Mon Dieu,*' said the
30 monarch to M. de Talleyrand, 'of course it would be a great misfortune, but if the Neapolitan cruisers were to capture and hang my poor Garibaldi he would have brought this sad fate upon himself. It would simplify things a good deal. What a fine monument he should get erected to him!'

35 That day, certainly, the King would have been easily consoled for the death of the Captain of the Thousand. The bold attempt succeeded, thanks to the courage and prestige of Garibaldi, greatly assisted by Neapolitan treason. Naples gave itself to Garibaldi, and Garibaldi offered his conquest to the King. But to anyone in Turin who has followed events
40 closely, it must be evident that, far from instigating and organising the invasion of the Two Sicilies, Cavour at least at first did try to oppose it. It was not till he realised that he could not possibly put a stop to the enterprise, outflanked as he had been by the Garibaldian war party, that he kept aloof, tolerating everything, and prepared to take advantage, as he
45 did, of a conquest he rightly considered dangerous and premature.

Denis Mack Smith (ed.), *The Making of Italy 1796–1866*, 1968, pp 332–4

Questions

a Is the view expressed by Henri d'Ideville of Victor Emmanuel's role in the creation of a united Italy a fair one?

* *b* Does recent research support d'Ideville's view of Victor Emmanuel's and Cavour's attitudes to Garibaldi in 1860? What explains their respective attitudes?

c How valuable is d'Ideville's testimony as historical evidence on the events and personalities to which he refers?

* *d* How important a part did popular support for the idea of national unity play in the events of 1859–61?

6 Mazzini writes to Giuseppe Ferretti, 25 August 1871

The Italy which we represent today, like it or not, is a living lie. Not only do foreigners own Italian territory on our frontiers with France and Germany, but, even if we possessed Trieste and Nice, we should still have only the material husk, the dead corpse of Italy. The life-giving touch of
5 God, the true soul of the nation, is lacking.

Italy was put together just as though it were a piece of lifeless mosaic, and the battles which made this mosaic were fought for reasons of calculating dynastic egoism by foreign rulers who should have been loathed as our natural enemies. Lombardy, scene of the great Five Days in

10 1848, allowed herself to be joined to Italy by the fiat of a French despot. The Venetians, despite their heroic defence in 1849, come to us by kind permission of a German monarch. The best of us once fought against France for possession of Rome; yet we remained the slaves of France so long as she was strong. Rome therefore had to be occupied furtively 15 when France lay prostrate at Germany's feet just because we feared to raise our ancient war cry against the Vatican. Southern Italy was won by volunteers and a real movement of the people, but then it resigned its early promise and abdicated to a government which still refuses to bestow on Italy a new national constitution.

20 The battles fought by Italy in this process were defeats. Custoza and Lissa were thus lost because of the ineptitude or worse of our leaders. Italians are now a vassal people, without a new constitution that could express their will. We can therefore have no real national existence or international policy of our own. In domestic politics we are ruled by an 25 arbitrary violation of the law; administrative corruption has been elevated into a system; a narrow franchise means that we are governed by a few rich men who are powerless for good. Our army is not popularly based, and it is used only for internal repression. Rights of the press and of free association are fettered, and a corrupt political system inevitably is 30 bringing a slow but growing financial collapse. Abroad we waver as before between a servile attachment now to France now to Germany. The alliance with the people has been betrayed, and our relations with Europe have thrown morality overboard just as in the worst centuries of Italian decline.

35 Some of our party are indignant with what is happening; though many of them forget our splendid past traditions and are eager to copy the most ruinous foreign political systems based on force. Ordinary people, however, are disillusioned. They had watched with astonished presentiment of great things to come as Italy, once ruler of the civilised world, 40 began to rise again; but now they avert their gaze from what is happening and say to themselves: 'this is just the ghost of Italy.'

Denis Mack Smith (ed.), *The Making of Italy 1796–1866*, 1968, pp. 363–4

Questions

a Explain the following references: (i) 'the great Five Days in 1848' (lines 9–10); (ii) 'Custoza and Lissa' (lines 20–1).

b Why does Mazzini approve of the method by which only one of the following was added to create a united Italy: (i) Lombardy; (ii) the Venetians; (iii) Rome; (iv) Southern Italy (lines 9–19)?

* *c* Why does Mazzini believe that Italy is a 'living lie' (line 1) in 1871? Have any of the ideals of the Young Italy movement as expressed forty years before been realised?

* *d* Is Mazzini's critical view of the new Italy borne out by the subsequent history of the country up to 1914?

7 An Historian contrasts German and Italian Unification

The 1815 settlement of Europe was shaken to its foundations by the revolutions of 1848–9 and definitively destroyed by the unifications of Italy and Germany in 1861–70. In Germany the revolutions immediately revealed a profound conflict between liberal values and the
5 urge towards national independence and power, which prepared the ground for the sacrifice of liberalism by Bismarck's triumphantly militaristic concept of unification. In Italy no such open clash occurred between the liberal creed and the struggle for national independence: the unification of Italy was achieved by, and confirmed the survival of, a
10 liberal democracy, however fragile its structure, however limited its base.

Fundamental among the reasons which explain the differences in the process of formation of these two new states was the strength of the democratic initiative in Italy. By imposing themselves on the latter phase of the revolutions, after the failure of the moderates, the democrats
15 aroused a spirit of patriotism, which – if still not touching the vast mass of the peasantry – penetrated widely among the literate classes and the urban workers. That monarchical Piedmont was able to exploit this situation in the famous *decennio* was due to the radical transformation of the international scene and to the capacity of the most sensitive and
20 technically equipped liberal leader, Cavour, to learn from the lessons of the revolutions. The new fluidity of international relations, which resulted from the breakdown of the Concert of Europe, permitted the development of national intitiatives, even by war, provided they remained confined within the bounds of international diplomacy and so
25 avoided the dangers of uncontrollable revolutionary conflagrations. Cavour's determined enactment of the liberal programme of reforms offered an effective, modern alternative to the democratic initiative, and ultimately succeeded in diplomatizing the democratic revolutionary drive for unity. This fortunate coincidence of international and national
30 developments and this antagonism between democrats and moderates resulted in the – unexpected – unification of Italy. The new Italy emerged out of the basic conflict of the opposing patriotic forces and the personal hostility of their leaders, not out of what traditional historiography was long inclined to interpret as the complementary and implicitly harmo-
35 nious roles of the four 'heroic' leaders – Victor Emmanuel, Cavour, Garibaldi and Mazzini – walking arm-in-arm towards a preordained unified state.

Stuart Woolf, *A History of Italy 1700–1860*, 1979, pp 361–2

Questions

a What is meant by (i) 'the democratic initiative' (line 13); (ii) 'the famous *decennio*' (line 18)?

b What does Woolf see as the significance of the 1848 revolutions in determining the different forms which unification would take in Italy and Germany?

c What were the 'international and national developments' (lines 29–30) which coincided to bring about Italian unification in Woolf's view?

* *d* In what senses was Cavour the most 'technically equipped liberal leader' (lines 19–20)? Outline the 'liberal programme of reforms' which he pursued.

e What contrasts does Woolf make between older and more recent interpretations of Italian unification? How has the new view come about?

f What light does Woolf's argument throw on the relationship between the Risorgimento and the unification of Italy?

Further Work

a Contrast the contributions made by Mazzini, Cavour and Garibaldi towards the making of a united and independent Italy.

b 'The fate of Italy was decided by warfare and diplomacy rather than by a national revival.' Discuss.

c 'The precise relationship between the Risorgimento and the unification of Italy is exceedingly hard to determine.' How should an historian tackle the problem of reaching a balanced judgement on this question?

III Austria, Prussia and German Unity, 1848–66

Introduction

In the concluding extract in the previous section, Stuart Woolf pointed to the importance of the contrasting events of 1848–9 in Italy and Germany in determining the paths to unity which the new states would take. This section takes the story of German unification from the year of revolutions to the exclusion of Austria from German affairs after her defeat in 1866. Historians have debated whether political discontent or economic hardship did more to create a revolutionary situation in central Europe by 1848, but it was events in Paris in February which finally sparked off successful uprisings in Vienna and Berlin. With the old authorities in disarray, for a time German liberals seemed to hold a strong hand; hopes ran high that they might bring into existence a united Germany through parliamentary action.

In May 1848 a national assembly was convened at Frankfurt and the role of this body has been the focal point for historians studying this 'lost opportunity' in German history. It has been attacked for political naivety – Hamerow sums up this view of the members of the Frankfurt assembly along these lines that 'instead of standing their enemies up against the wall and shooting them, they lectured and discussed as if they were conducting a seminar in some provincial university'. On the other hand, the assembly has also been condemned by historians such as A. J. P. Taylor and Sir Lewis Namier for having been more concerned with national power than liberal principles. 'With 1848,' writes Namier, 'starts the German bid for power, for European predominance, for world dominion.'

However, the completeness of the initial success of the revolutions had created a false impression of the assembly's real strength. Its members faced impossible choices in the task that was expected of them as circumstances outside their control changed. The first problem was that in both political and social fields the reforms which the Frankfurt liberals wished to see accompanying unification were strictly limited. Recent research by Donald J. Mattheisen (*Central European History*, June 1979) has confirmed the picture of the difficult position in which they found themselves. By analysing the voting records of the Frankfurt assembly on such matters as the extent of the suffrage and the relationship of parliament to the head of state in the new Germany, Mattheisen reaches the conclusion that the moderate liberals were 'at least as strongly opposed to democracy as they were to the old regime' and that they were anxious to keep monarchical authority as a safeguard against social revolution. As the governments of Austria and Prussia began to recover, the German liberals found themselves caught between revolution and reaction. Professor Ebenstein comments: 'Two-front wars can be as disastrous in social as in military history. That was the deepest cause of the failure of German liberalism in 1848–9.'

The second dilemma which faced the Frankfurt assembly was the territorial extent of the new state, the alternatives being the *Grossdeutsch* or *Kleindeutsch* solutions – the inclusion or exclusion of Austria's German provinces. Again, the recovery of Austria meant that by 1849 the Frankfurt assembly could only try to put into effect the *Kleindeutsch* variant. Frederick William's rejection of the offer of the crown of Germany, however, simply confirmed the failure of the liberal bid for national unity.

Austria was again dominant in Germany for a short period after 1849. However, in the face of Prussian opposition, she was unable to strengthen her hand in the vital field of economic relations with the German states. Errors of foreign and domestic policy in the 1850s, culminating in defeat by France in 1859, meant that her strength ebbed vis-à-vis Prussia. Although in 1848–9 the imperial government had survived by playing off the races of the empire against each other, unsuccessful attempts to resolve the problem of the nationalities left Austria gravely weakened. By way of contrast, as Professor Grenville points out, Prussia's internal problems were political ones which Bismarck showed could be overcome by exploiting the strength of national feeling. When Bismarck began to impose his 'blood and iron' solution on the problem of unification, it was at the expense not only of Austria but also of the parliamentary future of Germany – a theme which will be taken up again in section VIII.

Further Reading

The best general surveys as background for this section are Agatha Ramm, *Germany 1789–1919* (Methuen, 1967) and C. A. Macartney, *The Habsburg Empire 1790–1918* (Weidenfeld & Nicolson, 1968). Further documents can be found in H. Böhme (ed.), *The Foundation of the German Empire: Select Documents* (Oxford University Press, 1971) and for the economic aspects of the subject see T. S. Hamerow, *Restoration, Revolution, Reaction: Economics and Politics in Germany 1815–71* (Princeton University Press, 1958). Different views on the place of the 1848 revolutions in German history can be studied in Viet Valentin, *1848: Chapters of German History* (Allen & Unwin, 1940), Sir Lewis Namier, *1848: The Revolution of the Intellectuals* (Oxford University Press, 1944), F. Eyck, *The Frankfurt Parliament 1848–9* (Macmillan, 1968) and P. N. Stearns, *The Revolutions of 1848* (Norton, 1974). The 'Problems in European Civilization' volume, Melvin Kranzberg, *1848: A Turning Point?* (D. C. Heath & Co., 1959) is now widely available, having been made an Open University set book. A. J. P. Taylor's three books, *The Course of German History* (Hamish Hamilton, 1945), *The Habsburg Monarchy* (Hamish Hamilton, 1948) and *The Struggle for Mastery in Europe 1848–1918* (Clarendon Press, 1954) are, of course, indispensable reading. For further books on Bismarck's role, see section VIII.

1 Prince Hohenlohe's Memorandum on the Condition of Germany written at the end of 1847

In the history of every nation there is an epoch in which it comes to full self-consciousness, and claims liberty to determine its own destiny. . . . We in Germany have reached this stage. The nation demands a share in public administration now as never before. The Governments, however, 5 reject this movement. In it they see, or wish to see, only the propaganda of a radical clique, and they are filled with misgivings. One reason for discontent is universally diffused in Germany; every thinking German is deeply and painfully aware of it. This is the impotence of Germany among other states. Let no one say that Austria and Prussia as great 10 powers represent the might of Germany in her foreign relations. On the one hand Austria asserts herself far too little because she is lacking in internal strength; on the other, Prussia, to speak plainly, is only admitted on sufferance among the great powers, and will not hold even this position much longer if the movement in internal politics continues as it 15 has begun. In last resort, however, there are only Austria and Prussia, while the rest of Germany for ever plays a minor part as a mere camp-follower. No one will deny that it is hard on a thinking, energetic man to be unable to say abroad: 'I am a German' – not to be able to pride himself that the German flag is flying from his vessel, to have no German Consul 20 in cases of emergency, but to have to explain, 'I am a Hessian, a Darmastädter, a Bückeburger; my Fatherland was once a great and powerful country, now it is shattered into eight-and-thirty splinters.' And when we study the map and see how the Baltic, and North Sea, and the Mediterranean break upon our shores, and how no German flag 25 commands the customary salute from the haughty French and English, surely the hue of shame alone will survive from the red, black and yellow, and mount our cheeks? . . . The industry so largely fostered by the *Zollverein* no longer suffices for our commerce in its present great extension, our rich trade seeks extraneous markets and connections over 30 sea. The outcry at the deficiencies of the German fleet, and the question of the unity of Germany – a real, politically efficacious unity – will be handled with fresh vigour by the now emancipated press.

Memoirs of Prince Chlodwig of Hohenlohe, 1906, vol I, pp. 40–1

Questions.

a Explain the following: (i) 'eight-and-thirty splinters' (line 22); (ii) 'the red, black and yellow' (line 26).

b What does Hohenlohe mean by 'the movement in internal politics' (line 14) in Prussia?

c Explain why the disunity of Germany distresses Hohenlohe. What do Hohenlohe's views tell us about the nature of German nationalism in the mid-nineteenth century?

* *d* 'One reason for discontent is universally diffused in Germany' (lines 6–7). How far was German nationalism a factor in causing the 1848 revolutions?

* *e* Explain the significance of the *Zollverein* (line 28) in German affairs before 1848.

2 Frederick Engels on the Frankfurt Parliament, from an article in the New York Tribune, 27 February 1852

After the popular victories of Vienna and Berlin, it was a matter of course that there should be a Representative Assembly for all Germany. This body was consequently elected, and met at Frankfurt . . . .This Assembly of old women was, from the first day of its existence, more
5 frightened of the least popular movement than of all the reactionary plots of all the German Governments put together. . . . We had the strange spectacle of an Assembly pretending to be the only legal representative of a great and sovereign nation, and yet never possessing the will or the force to make its claims recognised. The debates of this body, without any
10 practical result, were not even of any theoretical value, reproducing, as they did, nothing but the most hackneyed commonplace themes of superannuated philosophical and juridical schools. . . .

The people of Germany, deeply feeling the necessity of doing away with the obnoxious territorial division that scattered and annihilated the
15 collective force of the nation, for some time expected to find, in the Frankfurt National Assembly at least, the beginning of a new era. But the childish conduct of that set of wiseacres soon disenchanted the national enthusiasm. The disgraceful proceedings occasioned by the armistice of Malmo made the popular indignation burst out against a body which, it
20 had been hoped, would give the nation a fair field for action, and which, instead, carried away by unequalled cowardice, only restored to their former solidity the foundations upon which the present counter-revolutionary system is built.

Frederick Engels, *Germany: Revolution and Counter-Revolution*, 1969, pp. 50–3

Questions

* *a* Who was Frederick Engels?

* *b* How was the 'Representative Assembly' elected in 1848? Why was Frankfurt chosen as its location?

* *c* Compare Engels' vision of the changes which national unity would bring about with Hohenlohe's views expressed in the previous extract.

* *d* Explain the reference to the armistice of Malmo (line 19). How did it affect the position of the Frankfurt assembly?

* *e* What explanation does Engels give for the failure of the Frankfurt assembly? What other factors does he not take into account?

* *f* Did anything of value emerge from the discussions of the Frankfurt assembly?

3 Frantisek Palacky replies in April 1848 to an Invitation to attend the Frankfurt Assembly as a Czech Delegate

I am a Czech of Slav descent and with all the little I own and possess I have devoted myself wholly and for ever to the service of my nation . . . .

You know that in south-east Europe, along the frontiers of the Russian Empire, there live many nations widely different in origin, language,
5 history and habits – Slavs, Rumanians, Magyars, and Germans, not to speak of Greeks, Turks and Albanians – none of whom is strong enough by itself to be able to resist successfully for all time the superior neighbour to the east; they could do it only if a close and firm tie bound them all together . . . . Certainly, if the Austrian state had not existed for ages, we
10 would be obliged in the interests of Europe and even of mankind to endeavour to create it as fast as possible.

But why have we seen this state, which by nature and history is destined to be the bulwark and guardian of Europe against the Asiatic element of every kind – why have we seen it in a critical moment helpless
15 and almost unadvised in the face of the advancing storm? It is because in an unhappy blindness which has lasted for very long, Austria has not recognised the real legal and moral foundation of its existence and has denied it: the fundamental rule that all the nationalities united under its sceptre should enjoy complete equality of rights and respect. . . . I am
20 convinced that even now it is not too late for the Austrian Empire to proclaim openly and sincerely this fundamental rule of justice. . . .

When I look behind the Bohemian frontiers, then natural and historical reasons make me turn not to Frankfurt but to Vienna to seek there the centre which is fitted and destined to ensure and defend the
25 peace, the liberty and the right of my nation. Your efforts, gentlemen, seem to me now to be directed as I have already stated, not only towards ruinously undermining, but even utterly destroying that centre from whose might and strength I expect the salvation not only of the Czech land.

Hans Kohn (ed.), *The Habsburg Empire 1804–1918*, 1961, pp. 118–22

Questions

* *a* Who was Frantisek Palacky and why was he invited to attend the Frankfurt assembly?
  b Why does Palacky believe that the existence of the Austrian empire is 'in the interests of Europe' (line 10)?
  c Why does Palacky turn down the invitation to attend the assembly?
* *d* Were Palacky's hopes for a new approach to the rights of the nationalities in the Austrian empire realised in the aftermath of the 1848 revolutions?
* *e* What light does Palacky's statement throw on the debates at Frankfurt over the *Kleindeutsch* and *Grossdeutsch* solution to the problem of German unification?

4 Frederick William IV and the Future of Germany, 1848–9

(a) The Revolution in Berlin, March 1848

In the course of the morning of the 21st the King appeared in the streets on horseback, with the German colours round his arm. He was greeted with tumultuous applause; and when he reached the University . . . he stopped near the monument of Frederick II, and, carried away by
5 uncontrollable excitement, said, 'I am truly proud that it is my capital where so powerful an opinion has manifested itself. This day is a great day. It ought never to be forgotten. . . . The colours I wear are not my own; I do not mean to usurp anything with them; I want neither another crown nor another dominion. I want liberty; I will have unity in
10 Germany; I want good order. I swear it before God. . . . I believe that the hearts of the princes yearn towards me, and that the will of the nation supports me. . . .'

In another proclamation the King said: 'From this day forth the name Prussia is fused and dissolved into that of Germany. The Diet which has
15 already been convoked for the 2nd of April, in conjunction with my people, presents the ready medium and legal organ for the deliverance and pacification of Germany.'

Annual Register 1848, pp. 380–1

(b) Frederick William IV writes to Baron von Radowitz, 23 December 1848

Here, as a final end, is a little word of confession about the crown which the *Paulskirche* has for sale: every German nobleman, who bears on his
20 coat of arms a cross or a bar, is a hundred times too good to accept such a diadem moulded out of the dirt and dregs of revolution, disloyalty and treason. The old, legitimate crown of the German nation, not worn since 1806, the diadem by divine right, which makes him who bears it the highest authority in Germany, which men obey for conscience's sake –

25 that crown one can accept if one feels one has the strength for it, and if one's own duties allow it. That crown, however, no one bestows except the Emperor Francis Joseph, myself, and our equals; and woe to him who accepts it, if the price is the loss of a third of Germany and the noblest sections of the German nation. God help us! Amen.

H. Böhme (ed.), *The Foundation of the German Empire: Select Documents*, 1971, pp 65–6

(c) Frederick William* IV*'s Reply to the Deputation from the Frankfurt Assembly which had offered him the Imperial Crown on 3 April 1849

30 Gentlemen, the message you bring me has deeply moved me . . . In the resolution you have communicated to me I recognise the voice of the representatives of the German people. Your call gives me a title, the value of which I know how to prize. If accepted, it demands from me incalculable sacrifices, and burdens me with heavy duties. The German 35 National Assembly has counted on me in all things which were calculated to establish the unity, power and glory of Germany. I feel honoured by their confidence; and I am ready by deeds to prove that their reliance on my fidelity, love and devotion to the cause of the country has not been misplaced; but I should not justify that confidence – I should not answer 40 to the expectations of the German people – if I, violating sacred rights and breaking my former explicit and solemn promises, were, without the voluntary assent of the crowned Princes and free States of our Fatherland, to take a resolution which must be of decisive importance to them and to the States which they rule. It will now lie with the several Governments 45 of the German States to examine the constitution which the National Assembly has drawn up, and declare whether it will be of advantage to all – whether the rights it confers on me will place me in the position to guide the destinies of Germany and realise the expectations of the people. But of this Germany may be certain, and you may declare it in every 50 State – that if it needs the protection of the Prussian sword I will, even without a summons, not hesitate to follow that course from which my royal House has never departed – the course of fidelity and honour.

Annual Register 1849, pp 347–8

Questions

a Explain the following: (i) 'The Diet . . . Germany' (lines 14–17); (ii) 'the *Paulskirche*' (line 19); (iii) 'The old . . . 1806' (lines 22–3).

* *b* How far were Frederick William's comments about the 'hearts of the princes' and the 'will of the nation' (lines 10–11) justified in 1848?

c What reasons does Frederick William give in extract (b) for his hostility to the Frankfurt assembly? Explain the reference to 'the loss of a third of Germany' (line 28).

d What reasons does Frederick William give in extract (c) for not accepting the imperial crown? Do you think these were his real motives?

e What picture of Frederick William and of his attitudes to the future of Prussia and German unification emerges from these three extracts?

* *f* Who was Baron von Radowitz to whom Frederick William is writing in extract (b)? What plan did he devise for the reorganisation of Germany after the failure of the Frankfurt assembly and what was the outcome?

5 The Significance of 1848 in German History: the Views of Two Historians

(a) The year 1848 was the turning point at which modern history failed to turn. The military despotisms of Central Europe were nearly but not quite transformed by a timely and natural action of domestic forces. It was the appointed hour, but the despotisms just succeeded in surviving it, and modernised their methods without altering their essential character. The misfortunes of European civilisation in our own day sprang in no small degree from those far-off events. . . . In 1848 Germany was anti-liberal, if not in heart and mind, at least in energy and will. The Parliament of Frankfurt, which was to have united her, lacked the powerful spirit of Pym or Franklin, of Mirabeau or of Cavour. If the King of Prussia would not, Germany could not. Her men of genius and her instincts for action were dedicated to other ideals. She was destined to be united, not in 1848 on a basis of freedom, but in 1866 and 1870 on a basis of military Kaiserdom. The failure of 1848 permanently to overturn military despotism in the centre of the Continent was fatal to the healthy development of Europe as a whole.

George Macaulay Trevelyan, *British History in the Nineteenth Century and After*, 1937, pp 292–4

(b) Failure or not, 1848 was a genuine turning point. . . . In recalling 1848, we recall a divide. In terms of political history this may amount to a truism; even abortive revolutions are bound to have profound effects. The year 1850 no more restored the status of 1847 than 1815 had returned to 1788. . . . However brief the constitutional experiments of 1848–49 had been, in some of the countries concerned they resulted in the strengthening of state unity and the leveling of regional or social inequalities. They left behind universal manhood suffrage as a great legacy of the continental revolution. Forty-eight . . . was the most important year for the whole of Europe's constitutional life. Upon none of the reborn autocratic regimes were the liberal and democratic experiments altogether lost. . . . The historian cannot overlook the fact that revolutions are conducive to evil as well as to good. . . . German liberals of 1848 . . . wore the blinkers of their own time. But in principle history has confirmed their view that the deification of the masses is no sounder political tenet than the deification of the state and that liberty can be threatened from two sides.

Hans Rothfels, '1848 – One Hundred Years After', *Journal of Modern History*, 1948, pp 293–4, 306

Questions

a Explain what is meant by (i) 'Her men . . . other ideals' (lines 11–12); (ii) 'a truism' (line 19).

b Trevelyan and Rothfels both describe 1848 as a 'turning point'. Explain how they develop this idea in different ways in these extracts.

c Explain how Rothfels' judgement on liberalism in Germany in 1848 is more favourable than that of Trevelyan.

d In the light of Rothfels' comments, discuss Trevelyan's view that national unity in 1848 would have been achieved 'on a basis of freedom'.

* *e* With reference to the views expressed by Trevelyan and Rothfels, in what ways do you think Austria and Prussia were changed by the experience of the 1848 revolutions?

6 Count von Blome, Austrian envoy in Munich, writes to Alexander von Mensdorf-Poilly, Austrian Foreign Minister, 29 October 1864

Your Excellency takes over the conduct of affairs at a sad time and at a moment when Austria's reputation abroad, alas, is too low. . . . Perhaps it will afford you some little interest to know the unprejudiced (as I believe) judgement reached here, outside Austria, from a conscientious
5 observation of things. Our influence has sunk, not for the reason that we have embarked upon this or that specific course, nor because we have fought for Denmark's integrity, nor because we are allied to Prussia, or have opposed the Liberal opinions of the day. . . . We have lost reputation and sympathy just because we follow no specific
10 policy. . . . We are no longer credited with the necessary firmness to strive persistently either for a traditional or a new aim. We are seen to vacillate; we are no longer feared; we are, therefore, less popular. Lasting popularity is never won by concessions to public opinion. The policy of the *Furstentag* [Congress of Princes 1863] was a great one – had we
15 carried it through energetically and consistently. We dropped it. It would be an egregious mistake, in my opinion, to return to it now, or a variant of it, and only to court the alliance of the German medium-sized and small states. The medium-sized states will always come to us when they need us, and they can only need us when we are powerful. They on their
20 side afford us no support, as 1859 showed. We must now turn the alliance with Prussia to good account. . . . Of course Bismarck has hitherto taken the lion's share of advantage from that connection; of course Prussia will always seek to drive us out of Germany; we can only fight Prussia if we combine with France, and, since we do not wish to do that, our task is to

25 prevent Prussia from falling into her arms. It will be easy for us to counteract the disadvantageous results of the commercial treaty with France if we decidedly turn to the system of free trade, for the future belongs to it and we cannot escape it. We shall also find in it the most effective means of fusing England's interests with ours. Moreover,
30 England is neither an active ally nor a decided enemy. Russia, for years to come, will have to observe a passive attitude. Our course in relation to Italy, and especially Rome, is so prescribed by tradition, principles, feeling, and interests that we cannot abandon it without ruining ourselves. In Germany it is time to cease to meddle and muddle. Where
35 we neither wish to bite nor can do so.

H. Böhme (ed.), *The Foundation of the German Empire: Select Documents*, 1971, pp 132–3

Questions

a Explain the following: (i) 'we have fought for Denmark's integrity' (lines 6–7); (ii) 'They on their side . . . showed' (lines 19–20); (iii) 'the commercial treaty with France' (lines 26–7)?

b What does von Blome see as the fundamental reason for the decline in Austria's position in Europe?

* *c* What was the 'policy of the *Furstentag*' (lines 13–14)? Why in fact did it fail?

d How convincingly does von Blome set out his case for a new course in Austrian policy?

* *e* 'In 1850 Prussian policy had seemed to end in complete failure. Within a decade Prussia was on the threshold of complete success.' Account for this apparently dramatic reversal.

7 Count Karolyi, Austrian ambassador in Berlin, writes to Count Alexander von Mensdorf-Poilly, 22 February 1866

So far, during the whole course of the Duchies question, the differences between the two Powers have been limited to the Cabinets. They have now been transplanted to the field of public opinion. . . . I should like to think that this artificial exaggeration of the danger by public opinion
5 formed an essential part of the calculations and actions of Count Bismarck. If the purpose of his policy is to bring the Duchies question quickly to a definitive solution in a specifically Prussian sense, it is to his interest to win public opinion, through the Press. . . . I am clear that Count Bismarck no longer intends a mere attempt at intimidation for the
10 attainment of his purposes (he may have limited himself to this in the various previous phases of the Gastein Convention), if he does not succeed, at least in a partial furthering of his policy. He holds that the time has come to mount a great Prussian action abroad and, if it can be done in

no other way, to appeal to the arbitrament of war, and he thinks that
15 circumstances are favourable for this. Such an action has been from the beginning the goal of his political career. It would suitably quiet his ungoverned and unscrupulous, but daring, thirst for achievement.

Count Bismarck considers the annexation of the Duchies, or something approaching it, a matter of life and death for his political existence
20 and he seeks to make it appear such for Prussia too. After such a success, especially if it were attained by means of a fortunate war, the Government would more easily master the internal strife. Its end without the diversion of war would be subject to the most critical difficulties; for it is absolutely inconceivable that King
25 William could bring about legal recognition of the principles represented by his Government without a coup d'état. His Majesty is supposed to have positively refused his consent to the coup d'état, which Count Bismarck may well have recommended. The most effective, indeed the only means, of bringing about a sudden change internally must be thus
30 sought in the field of foreign policy. It is such points of view which guide Bismarckian policy.

H. Böhme (ed.), *The Foundation of the German Empire: Select Documents*, 1971, p 161

Questions

a Explain the following: (i) 'the Duchies question' (line 1); (ii) 'in a specifically Prussian sense' (line 7); (iii) 'the Gastein Convention' (line 11).

b Why does Karolyi regard the situation between Prussia and Austria as having taken an ominous turn?

c What does Karolyi see as Bismarck's motives for moving towards war with Austria?

* *d* '[H]e thinks that circumstances are favourable'. Explain how a situation favourable to military action by Prussia had come about in 1866.

* *e* Do you think Karolyi's judgement on Bismarck is acceptable: 'Such an action has been from the beginning the goal of his political career' (lines 15–6)?

8 Bismarck urges the King of Prussia to make an Early Peace with Austria, 24 July 1866

We had to avoid wounding Austria too severely; we had to avoid leaving behind in her unnecessary bitterness of feeling or desire for revenge; we ought rather to reserve the possiblity of becoming friends again with our adversary of the moment, and in any case to regard the Austrian state as a
5 piece on the European chessboard and the renewal of friendly relations with her as a move open to us. If Austria were severely injured, she would

become the ally of France and of every other opponent of ours; she would even sacrifice her anti-Russian interests for the sake of revenge on Prussia.

On the other hand, I could see no future acceptable to us for the 10 countries constituting the Austrian monarchy, in case the latter were split up by risings of the Hungarians and Slavs or made permanently dependent on those peoples. What would be put in that portion of Europe which the Austrian state from Tyrol to the Bokowina had hitherto occupied? Fresh formations on this surface could only be of a 15 permanently revolutionary nature. German Austria we could neither wholly nor partly make use of. The acquisition of provinces like Austrian Silesia and portions of Bohemia could not strengthen the Prussian State; it would not lead to an amalgamation of German Austria with Prussia, and Vienna could not be governed from Berlin as a mere de- 20 pendency. . . . The prolongation of the war would pave the way for a French intervention. We must finish off rapidly; before France won time to bring further diplomatic action to bear upon Austria.

Bismarck: The Man and the Statesman, Being the Reflections and Reminiscences of Otto Prince von Bismarck, 1898, vol II, pp 48–50

Questions

a Summarise the arguments Bismarck uses here in urging the ending of the war between Prussia and Austria against the wishes of the king and the military leaders. What other factors might have influenced him which he would not have referred to in these circumstances?

b What do Bismarck's comments on the question of territorial acquisitions at the expense of Austria suggest about his attitude to German nationalism in 1866?

* *c* Did Bismarck's arguments expressed here have the desired effect in 1866? What were the terms of the peace with Austria?

* *d* What effect did the Prussian victory have on internal problems in Prussia and Austria?

Further Work

a How were the interests of Austria and Prussia obstacles to the development of German unity in the period 1815 to 1850?

b Was the failure of the revolutions of 1848 in Austria and Germany due to the mistakes of the liberals?

c Did the events of 1848–9 do anything to advance the cause of German unity?

d How far did the events of 1848–9 in Austria and Germany determine the nature of the movement for German unity in the 1850s and 1860s?

IV Russia under Alexander II: the Emancipation of the Serfs, 1861

Introduction

This section looks at why and how the emancipation of the serfs came about in Russia in 1861, and the effects of this reform and those which followed from it on the political, social and economic life of the country. Four of the extracts are taken from memoirs of the period. A number of important points need to be considered in weighing up the value of memoirs as historical evidence on particular events. The author's age when the events took place and the date at which the memoirs were written are significant, as both understanding and memory affect the reliability of an account. Secondly, the authors of memoirs write with the benefit of hindsight and a knowledge of the course of events which could have coloured their recollections is essential. Thirdly, information on the writer's background and beliefs, if available, can help to identify prejudice and bias, either intentional or unintentional. Finally, it is important to consider how far the information and opinions contained in memoirs are based on personal experience and how much on knowledge acquired at second-hand.

In analysing the possible causes which led to emancipation in 1861, it has been argued that there was a 'revolutionary' situation in Russia at the end of the Crimean war and that fear for the immediate future was the mainspring of the movement for reform. This overstates the case, but there is little doubt that the war, coinciding with the opening of a new reign, was the catalyst for emancipation. Serfdom had been seen as a guarantee of Russia's stability and strength. Now, as liberal ideas were challenging the morality of the institution, the Crimean war had cast doubt on serfdom as the basis for national security. The commander-in-chief in the Crimea, Prince Gorchakov, described serfdom as 'the knot which binds together all the things that are evil in Russia'.

Emancipation eventually came about in 1861 through a mixture of local action and central direction. Tsar Alexander's role was crucial in determining that fears of the consequences of emancipation would not override the need for reform and that it would be achieved with the semblance of support from the landowners. On the latter point the question whether serfdom was widely seen to be undesirable from an economic as well as a moral and political point of view has been debated by historians. However, there was clearly not a serious enough economic crisis to overcome the conservatism of the vast majority of the landowners. As Aleksei Levshin, assistant minister of internal affairs from 1856–9, wrote, 'A genuine appeal to free the serfs, an appeal based on real conviction, did not come from any *guberniia* at all.' Pressure from the tsar, rather than economic self-interest, was the stimulus for the local initiatives.

The emancipation, in Seton-Watson's words, 'created more problems than it solved'. From the outset there was widespread discontent amongst the peasants. On 2 December 1861, Lanskoi, the minister of internal affairs, had to issue a circular refuting the idea that a further emancipation was due giving the peasants 'new privileges'. Economically, the emancipation may have done something to stimulate economic growth in Russia, but as M. E. Falkus observes, many of its features at a time of great population increase had a serious retarding effect. The inadequacy of the grants of land to the peasants, the heavy 'redemption' payments and the powers given to the commune or *mir* restricted the free movement of labour, agricultural innovation and individual prosperity. Nearly twenty years to the day after emancipation, the statement issued by the revolutionaries responsible for the Tsar's assassination in 1881 declared, 'After emancipating the peasants, the Government has given them into the hands of the nobles and speculators; the only consequence of the so-called reforms has been that people are sinking more and more into slavery and poverty.'

At the end of the Crimean war the tsar had said, 'The peace is signed; we must profit by it.' There followed the emancipation edict, local government reforms, changes in the legal and educational systems and the introduction of compulsory military service. As Richard Pipes says, this formed 'the most ambitious effort in Russian history to bring society into active participation in national life short of allowing it to share in the political process'. Perhaps this exclusion and the apathy it engendered, not serfdom as Prince Gorchakov had thought, was the real 'knot' in the Russian system. As opposition to the regime and terrorist violence grew, Miliutin, the war minister, wrote on 22 January 1880, 'It is hard to root out the evil when not in a single layer of society does the government encounter either sympathy or true support.' A glimmer of light from the plans for political reform drawn up by General Boris Melikov was extinguished by the Tsar's assassination and the reaction that inevitably followed.

Further Reading

The two best standard works on Russian history in the nineteenth century as a whole are M. T. Florinsky, *Russia: A History and an Interpretation* (Macmillan, 1947) and Hugh Seton-Watson, *The Russian Empire 1801–1917* (Clarendon Press, 1967). For further documentary coverage, see George Vernadsky (ed.), *A Source Book for Russian History from Early Times to 1917* (Yale University Press, 1972), volume III. W. E. Moose, *Alexander II and the Modernisation of Russia* (English

Universities Press, 1958) looks at all aspects of the reign, including foreign policy. With regard to the emancipation of the serfs, the social and economic aspects are covered by J. Blum, *Lord and Peasant in Russia from the Ninth to the Nineteenth Century* (Princeton University Press, 1961), M. E. Falkus, *The Industrialisation of Russia 1700–1914* (Macmillan, 1972) (see extract 6 below) and Richard Pipes, *Russia under the Old Regime* (Weidenfeld & Nicolson, 1974). An interesting study of the political processes involved in the emancipation is Daniel Field, *The End of Serfdom: Nobility and Bureaucracy in Russia 1855–61* (Harvard University Press, 1976). Arthur Adams, *Imperial Russia after 1861 – Peaceful Modernisation or Revolution?* (D. C. Heath & Co., 1965) looks at historians' views of economic, political and ideological problems in Russia leading up to the revolution.

1 Tsar Alexander's Speech in the State Council, 28 January 1861

The matter of the liberation of the serfs, which has been submitted for the consideration of the State Council, I consider to be a vital question for Russia, upon which will depend the development of her strength and power. I am sure that all of you, gentlemen, are just as convinced as I am
5 of the benefits and necessity of this measure. I have another conviction, which is that this matter cannot be postponed; therefore I demand that the State Council finish with it in the first half of February so that it can be announced before the start of the work in the fields. . . .

For four years now it has dragged on and has been arousing various
10 fears and anticipations among both the estate owners and the peasants. Any further delay could be disastrous to the state. I cannot help being surprised and happy, and I am sure all of you are happy, at the trust and calm shown by our good people in this matter. Although the apprehensions of the nobility are to a certain extent understandable, for the closest
15 and material interests of each are involved, notwithstanding all this, I have not forgotten and shall never forget that the approach to the matter was made on the initiative of the nobility itself, and I am happy to be a witness to this before posterity . . . . I hope, gentlemen, that on inspection of the drafts presented to the State Council, you will assure
20 yourselves that all that can be done for the protection of the interests of the nobility has been done: if on the other hand you find it necessary in any way to alter or to add to the presented work, then I am ready to receive your comments; but I ask you only not to forget that the basis of the whole work must be the improvement of the life of the peasants – an
25 improvement not in words alone or on paper but in actual fact. . . .

My late father was continuously occupied with the thought of freeing the serfs. Sympathising completely with this thought, already in 1856, before the coronation, while in Moscow I called the attention of the leaders of the nobility of the Moscow *guberniia* to the necessity for them

30 to occupy themselves with improving the life of the serfs, adding that serfdom could not continue for ever and that it would therefore be better if the transformation took place from above rather than from below. . . .

The Editorial Commissions worked for a year and seven months and, notwithstanding all the reproaches, perhaps partly just, to which the 35 commissions were exposed, they finished their work conscientiously and presented it to the Main Committee. The Main Committee, under the chairmanship of my brother, toiled with indefatigible energy and zeal. I consider it my duty to thank all the members of the committee, especially my brother, for their conscientious labours in this matter.

George Vernadsky (ed.). *A Source Book for Russian History from Early Times to 1917*, 1972, vol III, p 599

Questions

a What reasons does Alexander give to the state council for wishing to see the problem of serfdom speedily resolved?

b Comment on Alexander's statement about his father (lines 26–7).

c What was a '*guberniia*' (line 29)? What effect did Alexander's speech to the Moscow *guberniia* have?

* *d* '[T]he approach to the matter was made on the initiative of the nobility itself' (lines 16–7). How valid is this statement? Why was it important for Alexander to promote this version of events?

* *e* Explain the role of the editorial commissions and the main committee in drawing up the emancipation edict. What reproaches might Alexander have thought could justly be made of the former?

* *f* What were the main provisions of the emancipation edict? Did the aims of the 'protection of the interests of the nobility' and the 'improvement of the life of the peasants' prove to be incompatible?

2 The Abolition of Serfdom – Recollections of Prince Peter Kropotkin

[At the time of the emancipation, Prince Kropotkin, born in 1842, was a student in the Corps of Pages, a select military school attached to the imperial court in St Petersburg. He was subsequently imprisoned for his political views but escaped and fled abroad, where he published his autobiography.]

The revolution of 1848 had had its distinct echo in the hearts of the Russian peasant folk, and from the year 1850 the insurrections of revolted serfs began to take serious proportions. When the Crimean War broke out, and militia was levied all over Russia, these revolts spread with a 5 violence never before heard of. . . . These outbreaks on the one side, and the profound aversion to serfdom which had grown up in the generation which came to the front with the advent of Alexander II to the throne, rendered the emancipation of the peasants more and more imperative. The emperor, himself averse to serfdom, and supported, or rather influenced, in his own family by his wife, his brother Constantine, and the grand duchess Hélène Pávlovna, took the first steps in that direction. . . .

The attitude of the peasants was very remarkable. No sooner had the news spread that the liberation long sighed for was coming than the insurrections nearly stopped. . . . But after these moments of general rejoicing years of incertitude and disquiet followed. Specially appointed committees in the provinces and at St Petersburg discussed the proposed liberation of the serfs, but the intentions of Alexander II seemed unsettled. . . . There was no lack of young men amongst the nobility who earnestly worked for a frank abolition of the old servitude; but the serfdom party drew closer and closer round the emperor, and got power over his mind. They whispered into his ears that the day serfdom was abolished the peasants would begin to kill the landlords wholesale, and Russia would witness a new Pugachoff uprising, far more terrible than that of 1773. Alexander, who was a man of weak character, only too readily lent his ear to such predictions. But the huge machine for working out the emancipation law had been set to work. . . . I remember how the officers of the Horse Guards, whom I saw on Sundays, after the church parade at the home of my cousin used to side with Chernyshevsky, the leader of the advanced party in the emancipation struggle. The whole disposition of St Petersburg in the drawing-rooms and in the street, was such that it was impossible to go back. . . .

However, the party of the old nobility were not discouraged. . . . Things assumed a very gloomy aspect. The question whether the liberation would take place at all was now asked. I feverishly followed the struggle, and every Sunday, when my comrades returned from their homes, I asked them what their parents said. By the end of 1860 the news became worse and worse. 'The Valueff party has got the upper hand.' 'They intend to revise the whole work.' 'The relatives of the Princess X (a friend of the Tsar) work hard upon him.' 'The liberation will be postponed: they fear a revolution.'

In January 1861 slightly better rumours began to circulate. . . . On the last Sunday of the carnival (March 5, or rather March 17, new style), I was at the corps, having to take part in the military parade at the riding-school. I was still in bed, when my soldier servant, Ivanoff, dashed in with the tea tray, exclaiming, 'Prince, freedom! The manifesto is posted'. . . . I read and re-read the manifesto . . . serfdom was abolished, and the liberated serfs would get the land and their homesteads. They would have to pay for it, but the old stain of slavery was removed. They would be slaves no more; the reaction had *not* got the upper hand.

We went to the parade; and when all the military performances were over, Alexander II, remaining on horseback, loudly called out, 'The officers to me!' They gathered round him, and he began, in a loud voice, a speech about the great event of the day. 'The officers . . . the representatives of the nobility in the army' – these scraps of sentences reached our

55 ears – 'an end has been put to centuries of injustice . . . I expect sacrifices from the nobility . . . the loyal nobility will gather round the throne' . . . and so on. Enthusiastic hurrahs resounded amongst the officers as he ended. . . . The same enthusiasm was in the streets. Crowds of peasants and educated men stood in front of the palace, shouting hurrahs, and the
60 Tsar could not appear without being followed by demonstrative crowds running after his carriage. . . .

Where were the uprisings which had been predicted by the champions of slavery?. . . . Except in two places where there were insurrections, and a very few other spots where small disturbances entirely due to
65 misunderstandings and immediately appeased, took place – Russia remained quiet, more quiet than ever. . . .. I was in Nikolskoye [a Kropotkin family estate] in August 1861 and again in the summer of 1862, and I was struck with the quiet, intelligent way in which the peasants had accepted the new conditions. They knew perfectly well how
70 difficult it would be to pay the redemption tax for the land . . . but they so much valued the abolition of their personal enslavement that they accepted the ruinous charges – not without murmuring, but as a hard necessity – the moment that personal freedom was obtained.

Peter Kropotkin, *Memoirs of a Revolutionist*, London, 1899, vol I

Questions

a What evidence does this extract provide on the motives of those who were working for and against the abolition of serfdom? What does Kropotkin seem to regard as the chief benefit of emancipation?

* *b* Who were (i) Pugachoff (line 23); (ii) Chernyshevsky (line 28); (iii) Valueff (line 37)?

c What is Kropotkin's opinion of the tsar and the part he played in bringing about emancipation? Do you think his view is an objective one?

d What is Kropotkin's attitude to the Russian peasantry? Do you find his description of the peasants' reaction to the terms of the emancipation edict convincing?

e In the light of the points made about memoirs in the introduction to this section, how would you assess the value of this document as historical evidence?

3 The Abolition of Serfdom – Recollections of V.G. Korolenko

There must already have been talk at this time of the emancipation of the peasants. On one occasion Uncle Pyotr and someone else we knew expressed doubts as to whether 'the Tsar himself' could do everything he wished. 'Nicholas – he was a real Tsar. Everything trembled before him.

5 Yet how did he end?' My father replied with his usual saying, 'Hmm . . . It's way beyond us. If the Tsar wants to he'll do it.'

One year passed, and another. Rumours increased. . . . Everyone felt that something new was coming into our stagnant life, and every trifle was met anxiously, fearfully, keenly. By this time no trace remained of 10 my childhood impression of the immobility of the existing world. On the contrary, I felt that not only my own little world, but also the reaches far beyond the boundaries of the yard and the town, even Moscow and Petersburg were expecting something and were anxious about it. . . .

The Tsar wanted to take the peasants away from the landowners and 15 set them free. Was this good or bad? In our kitchen, as far as I can remember, they didn't expect anything good – perhaps because its membership was to some extent aristocratic. . . . To these people God had apportioned comparatively easy work, complete freedom from hunger and a fair amount of leisure in the warm kitchen. The unknown, 20 that was now near at hand, thus seemed to them in part alarming. 'Something's going to happen' – but whether it would be good or bad wasn't known. Anyway it was disturbing.

Such, however, was not the mood of our kitchen alone. Early one morning a large crowd of peasants appeared in our courtyard. . . . Soon 25 from above, from the lady's house, two old men without hats came down and said something to the crowd which had anxiously moved towards them. From the peasants there arose a quiet, apparently contented murmuring, and then the whole crowd knelt down: at the top of the stairway Mrs Kolyanovskaya had appeared, supported by attendant 30 maids. She was a stout, stately lady, with very alert black eyes, an aquiline nose and very obvious little black moustache. At the top of the steps, high above the kneeling crowd, surrounded by her staff, she seemed a queen among her subjects. She said a few gracious words, to which the crowd replied with a roar in which could be felt devotion and joy. At midday 35 they put tables up in the yard and regaled the peasants before their return.

I learned from the conversations of the adults that these were serfs of Kolyanovskaya, who had come from the distant village of Skolubov to ask that they be left as of old – 'we are yours, and you are ours.' Kolyanovskaya was a good mistress. The peasants had sufficient land, and 40 during the winter months almost all the workmen dispersed to various jobs. They, too, obviously lived better than their neighbours and 'something's going to happen' evoked in them the fear that this impending but unknown thing would 'equalize' them. . . .

Writers, when they write about that time, usually end with an 45 apotheosis of emancipation. Joyful and deeply moved crowds of people, incense, a prayer of thankfulness, hopes. I personally did not see anything like that, perhaps because I lived in a town. I certainly remember some official celebration – either on the occasion of the emancipation, or the announcement of the conquest of the Caucasus. Representatives of the 50 peasants had been driven to town to hear the manifesto read, and the evening before the streets were full of long peasant coats. There were a lot of peasants with medals, and also many women and children. This last circumstance is to be explained by the fact that an ominous rumour had spread among the people: the landowners had got the better of the Tsar, and again there would be no freedom. They were driving the peasants into the town and would shoot with field-guns. Among the squires, on the other hand, it was being said that it was unwise to gather such a mass of people in the town at such a time. This was discussed in our house too the day before the celebration. My father shrugged as usual. 'That's not our province.'

On the day of the celebration troops were positioned in the form of a square in the centre of the town. On one side shone a row of brass cannon, and the 'free' peasants lined up facing them. They gave an impression of sombre resignation to fate, and now and again would sigh heavily or start to lament. When, after the reading of some document or other, blanks were fired from the guns, hysterical shouts came from the crowd, which gave raise to a scene of great confusion. The women had thought they were starting to shoot the peasants. The old times had bequeathed to the new a part of their sad inheritance.

V.G. Korolenko, *The History of my Contemporary*, vol I, written about 1905; translated and abridged by Neil Parsons, 1972

[Korolenko, born in 1853, was the son of a senior Russian civil servant. He was imprisoned and twice exiled for his political activities. The extracts above take up the story in October 1858 when the tsar had just visited Korolenko's town.]

Questions

a Explain the following: (i) 'to some extent aristocratic' (line 17); (ii) 'an apotheosis of emancipation' (line 45); (iii) 'the conquest of the Caucasus' (line 49).

b What do these extracts tell us about the relationship between the tsar and his subjects?

c What are Korolenko's recollections of the attitude of the peasants to the possibility of emancipation and their reaction when it came? Why do you think he formed a different impression from Peter Kropotkin?

d Explain the meaning of the last sentence in this document.

e In the light of the points made about memoirs in the introduction to this section, how would you assess the value of this document as historical evidence?

4 The Abolition of Serfdom – Recollections of George Hume

Before Alexander II ascended the throne, the political life of Russia had been of so autocratic a character, that the whole country felt widespread

dissatisfaction, and was fully prepared to adopt more liberal ideas. . . . It became evident that, with the accession of Alexander II, a new era would
5 be inaugurated, and that a monarch had ascended the throne who had no sympathy whatever with the repressive system of his predecessor. It was at once obvious to the public that under Alexander II a complete transformation would be effected in the principles by which the country would be ruled, and in his first proclamation that he issued he appealed for
10 support to all classes of his people. . . .

The Crimean War is now generally considered to have been a great mistake on the part of England. To Russia, however, it was a great boon; it had certainly left her temporarily humiliated, but her unexpectedly gallant defence had gained for her the respect and sympathy, not only of
15 her late enemies, but of all civilised communities. This paved the way for the introduction, step by step, of those great reforms which have raised her in so short a time from a state of semi-barbarism to a co-equal voice with the other Great Powers in the destinies of Europe. It was the boom of the Allies' cannon that aroused her from her long sleep of apathetic
20 indolence and made possible the inception of those great reforms that characterised the reign of Alexander the Liberator.

The time has not yet arrived for a correct judgement to be formed of this monarch, and personally, with many others, I am of opinion that these developments followed too quickly for profitable assimilation, and thus
25 opened the path for the reactionary policy of his successor, Alexander III. . . .

Since 1857 I have had the opportunity of closely studying the sequence of reforms, which followed one another in quick succession. Thus, the great question of the land remained a constant cause of unrest amongst the
30 peasantry, who maintained that at the time of the emancipation under the will of the Emperor they were entitled to, and should have received without payment, all the land held by their proprietors. The publication of the Reform took place in the year 1861, but the Emancipation itself was only to be carried out at a two-years' interval in 1863. This the
35 peasantry did not understand, and it gave rise to many incidents of a most regrettable character, so much so that troops were quartered on the villages in order to compel them to go to work. . . .

It was from the balcony of M. Popoff's house that I heard him, surrounded by all the proprietors of the district, read out to his seven
40 thousand serfs, drawn up before his house according to their village, the Emperor's Ukase granting them their freedom. There they stood in serried rank, a picture of varied manhood in every stage of its development, from grey old age to early adolescence, as fine a body of men as you might wish to see. Standing without a smile, bare-headed
45 they listened with reverence to their Emperor's message, each mayor of the villages wearing his badge, and several the Emperor's coat that had been bestowed upon them for special service rendered to the State. Yet on the close of the ceremony there was no responsive cheer, and not the slightest enthusiasm on so momentous an occasion. It was evident from

50 their silence that they felt keen disappointment at no mention having been made that, together with their freedom, the whole land of the proprietors was to become the property of the late serfs. These representatives of the peasantry dispersed to their own villages evidently deeply depressed, and throughout all the years that have passed since then
55 they have been and are still fully convinced that the proprietors had not fulfilled their Emperor's commands.

George Hume, *Thirty-five Years in Russia*, London, 1914.

[George Hume, born in London in 1836, went to Russia in 1857 to sell agricultural machinery.]

Questions

a What is Hume's recollection of the peasants' reaction to emancipation? What reasons does he give to explain their attitude?

b What does this extract tell us about the relationship between the tsar, the landlords and the peasants in mid-nineteenth-century Russia?

* *c* How far does the way in which serfdom was abolished in 1861 justify Hume's view of the tsar's outlook and the political climate in Russia after the Crimean war?

* *d* '[T]hose great reforms' (line 16). Briefly outline the reforms carried out by Alexander II during his reign. How far were they necessitated by the abolition of serfdom?

e In the light of the points made about memoirs in the introduction to this section, how would you assess the value of this document as historical evidence?

5 The Abolition of Serfdom – Recollections of Sir Donald Mackenzie Wallace

About the time of the Crimean War, many of the landed proprietors had become alive to the necessity of improving the primitive traditional methods of agriculture, and sought for this purpose German stewards for their estates. . . . Immediately on his arrival, young Schmidt
5 [rechristened Karl Karl'itch by the Russians] had set himself vigorously to reorganise the estate and improve the method of agriculture. Some ploughs, harrows, and other implements which had been imported at a former period were dragged out of the obscurity in which they had lain for several years, and an attempt was made to farm on scientific principles.
10 The attempt was far from being completely successful, for the serfs – this was before the Emancipation – could not be made to work like regularly trained German labourers. In spite of all admonitions, threats and punishments, they persisted in working slowly, listlessly, inaccurately, and occasionally they broke the new instruments, from carelessness or
15 some more culpable motive.

When it became evident, in 1859, that the emancipation of the serfs was at hand, Karl Karl'itch confidently predicted that the country would inevitably go to ruin. He knew by experience that the peasants were lazy and improvident, even when they lived under the tutelage of a master, 20 and with the fear of the rod before their eyes. What would they become when this guidance and salutary restraint would be removed? The prospect raised terrible forebodings in the mind of the worthy steward, who had his employer's interests really at heart; and these forebodings were considerably increased and intensified when he learned that the 25 peasants were to receive by law the land which they occupied on sufferance, and which comprised about a half of the whole arable land of the estate. This arrangement he declared to be a dangerous and unjustifiable infraction of the sacred rights of property, which savoured strongly of communism, and could have but one practical result: the 30 emancipated peasants would live by the cultivation of their own land, and would not consent on any terms to work for their former master.

In the few months which immediately followed the publication of the Emancipation Edict in 1861, Karl Karl'itch found much to confirm his most gloomy apprehensions. The peasants showed themselves dissatisfied 35 with the privileges conferred upon them, and sought to evade the corresponding duties imposed on them by the new law. In vain he endeavoured, by exhortations, promises, and threats to get the most necessary part of the field-work done, and showed the peasants the provision of the law enjoining them to obey and work as of old until 40 some new arrangement should be made. To all his appeals they replied that, having been freed by the Tsar, they were no longer obliged to work for their former master; and he was at last forced to appeal to the authorities. This step had a certain effect, but the field-work was executed that year even worse than usual, and the harvest suffered in consequence.

45 Since that time things had gradually improved. The peasants had discovered that they could not support themselves and pay their taxes from the land ceded to them, and had accordingly consented to till the proprietor's fields for a moderate recompense. 'These last two years,' said Karl Karl'itch to me, with an air of self-satisfaction, 'I have been able after 50 paying all expenses, to transmit little sums to the young master in St Petersburg. It was certainly not much, but it shows that things are better than they were. Still, it is hard, uphill work. The peasants have not been improved by liberty. They now work less and drink more than they did in the times of serfage, and if you say a word to them, they'll go away and 55 not work for you at all.'

Sir Donald Mackenzie Wallace, *Russia*, 1877; revised and republished 1905

[Sir Donald was born in 1841 and spent many years travelling in Europe before becoming private secretary to the viceroys of India, and director of the foreign department of *The Times*. He lived in Russia 1870–5 and these extracts describe what he learned at the village of Ivanofka in 1870.]

Questions

a What do you think Sir Donald's source is for the information he gives here about Russian peasants and agriculture? How reliable is the source?

b Why did Karl Karl'itch object to the emancipation proposals? How far were his fears realised?

* *c* What do you learn from this extract about the problems of Russian agriculture before the emancipation? Did the terms of the emancipation improve the situation during the remainder of the nineteenth century?

d What is the relationship between landlord, peasants and steward on this estate? How does it compare with the estates with which Prince Kropotkin and V. G. Korolenko came into contact?

e In the light of the points made about memoirs in the introduction to this section, how would you assess the value of this document as historical evidence?

6 The Emancipation and Russian Industrial Development: an Historian's View

The Emancipation of the Serfs in 1861 removed a considerable barrier to industrial growth. Baykov[1], however, has suggested that serfdom should not be regarded as the principal obstacle to Russian economic development. He stresses that enough peasants were free of servile status
5 even before the Emancipation to provide a substantial industrial labour force. The presence of serf entrepreneurs and the development of freely hired *obrok* serfs may also warn us against exaggerating the restrictive elements of serfdom. Baykov emphasises rather the 'real' hindrances to Russian industrialisation: the vast distances and harsh climate, and the
10 inaccessibility of much of Russia's mineral wealth prior to the railway age.

On the other hand, serfdom was clearly incompatible with the requirements of an industrialising country. The basis of such a society was agriculture, and serfdom ensured a restricted home market and a low
15 level of agricultural technology. This in turn meant a low level of per capita incomes, which further perpetuated economic backwardness. Serfdom meant too a largely immobile population in which the level of education of the masses was abysmal. The simple pyramid structure of this stratified society, with its huge peasant base and small elite of landed
20 gentry, left little room for the development of a prosperous middle class. . . . Above all, perhaps, serfdom bred values and attitudes inimical to modernisation, and such values were not easily overcome in the post-

Emancipation period. Industrialisation, with the prospect of social upheaval that it entailed, was hardly likely to hold much appeal for the
25 landed classes. The greatly unequal distribution of the national income did not lead to the accumulation of savings by the wealthy for industrial development; rather, investment in land and in the acquisition of serfs was preferred. At the same time a high level of consumption of luxury goods (mostly imported) and large expenditures on foreign travel were
30 indulged in by many of the Russian aristocracy. The strong ties of the peasant to the land, too, were an enduring feature of Russian society throughout the nineteenth century. Gerschenkron[2] is surely right to stress the importance of Alexander II's great measure as a stimulus to Russian economic development, and indeed the year 1861 can in many
35 respects be taken as marking the beginning of Russia's modernisation. . . .

Yet while the retarding elements in serfdom on economic development are obvious, Gerschenkron has emphasised also the retarding features of the Reform itself. He points out that under the terms of the
40 Emancipation a prosperous peasant class was not created. In other words, the spur to industrialisation that might have come from the internal demand of a mass market remained lacking. Also, despite the poverty of the peasants, the Emancipation did not stimulate a flow of cheap labour to industrial occupations, and, allied to these points, agricultural produc-
45 tivity failed to show any significant increase, so that the rural sector continued backward and impoverished after 1861.

M. E. Falkus, *The Industrialisation of Russia 1700–1914*, 1972, pp 44–5, 47

1 A. Baykov, 'The Economic Development of Russia', *Economic History Review*, December 1954

2 A. Gerschenkron, 'Agrarian Policies and Industrialisation in Russia 1861–1917', *The Cambridge Economic History*, vol VI, part 2 (1966)

Questions

a Explain what is meant by (i) '*obrok* serfs' (line 7); (ii) 'per capita incomes' (lines 15–6).

b In what respects was serfdom 'incompatible with the requirements of an industrialising country' (lines 12–3)? What hindrances to Russian economic growth could not be blamed on serfdom?

c What does Falkus see as the 'values and attitudes' (line 21) caused by serfdom that militated against modernisation? How far did emancipation affect these?

d How did the terms in which the emancipation was framed have a 'retarding' effect on the prospects for industrial development in Russia?

* *e* In the first extract in this section the tsar speaks of the liberation of the serfs as being the key issue for the development of Russia's 'strength and power'. How far did emancipation give a boost to Russia's economic strength during the period up to 1914?

Further Work

a 'Experience shows that the most dangerous moment for a bad government is usually when it begins to reform itself' (Alexis de Tocqueville). Discuss why this should be so. Did the reforms of Alexander II's reign strengthen or weaken the tsarist regime in Russia?

b 'It was at once obvious to the public that under Alexander II a complete transformation would be effected in the principles by which the country would be ruled' (George Hume, document 4). How far was Russia of 1880 different from that of 1860?

c What are the strengths and weaknesses of autobiographies and memoirs as source material for historians? Illustrate your answer with examples taken from the above extracts.

V Louis Napoleon and the Second Empire

Introduction

Many statesmen devote their years in retirement to explaining to a sceptical world the underlying consistency of their many apparently inconsistent actions whilst in office. Louis Napoleon reversed the pattern. He put forward a set of principles for the government of France before he came to power, in political tracts such as *Des Idées Napoléoniennes* (1839) and *De L'Extinction du Paupérisme* (1844). His death in 1873 robbed him of the chance to attempt a *post mortem* on his own regime; by contrast, his uncle had helped to create his own legend whilst on St Helena. The relationship between Louis Napoleon's declared ideals and the events of his reign remains a matter of historical controversy. This chapter looks at some of the conflicting views of historians on this and other aspects of the Second Empire.

In his book *Napoléon-le-Petit*, published in 1852, Victor Hugo bitterly denounced Louis Napoleon as the 'pygmy tyrant of a great people', whose only purpose in seizing power was 'to have horses and mistresses, to be called Monseigneur, and to live well'. Such scathing attacks and the foreign policy disasters of the later years of the Second Empire helped dispose many writers to dismiss Napoleon III as a foolhardy adventurer, lacking in principles and judgement. Yet not all Louis Napoleon's contemporaries agreed with Victor Hugo's verdict – as can be seen from the first extract in this section – and historians too have come to see more positive aspects to his regime. It has been argued that his concern with the economic and social problems of France, his desire to bring peace and the triumph of the principle of nationality to Europe, and his intention to give his countrymen a more liberal form of government were genuine and far-sighted.

However, in the aftermath of the Second World War and the defeat of fascism in Europe, the idea that Napoleon III was a man ahead of his time gave rise to a fresh indictment. In 1933 a Nazi writer, Franz Kemper, had declared, 'The rise to power of Louis Napoleon is the only historical parallel to the National Socialist revolution of our day.' Sir Lewis Namier (see document 6) took up this theme and condemned Louis Napoleon's regime, based as he saw it on the fraudulent manipulation of the masses, as the forerunner of the fascist dictatorships. A. J. P. Taylor summed up this line of thought: 'There is nothing new in Hitler or Mussolini: Louis

Napoleon had all their cards up his sleeve, except, perhaps, their brutality.'

Subsequently historians have expanded the qualifying note at the end of that quotation to stress that Napoleon III had neither the inclination nor the means to regiment every aspect of the life of the state in the manner of twentieth-century totalitarian regimes. 'Of all his inconsistencies,' writes Paul Farmer in the *New Cambridge Modern History*, 'none was more excusable.' In his sympathetic study of the emperor published in 1961, T. A. B. Corley suggested that there was a closer parallel between Louis Napoleon and General de Gaulle. But though such comparisons between the past and the present may stimulate the reader's interest, it is arguable whether they lead to a greater historical understanding of a complex personality and the world in which he ruled.

Further Reading

A further selection of historians' views on Napoleon III can be found in Samuel M. Osgood (ed.), *Napoleon* III *and the Second Empire* (D. C. Heath & Co., 1973). Biographies of the emperor include J. M. Thompson, *Louis Napoleon and the Second Empire* (Blackwell, 1954), T. A. B. Corley, *Democratic Despot: A Life of Napoleon* III (Barrie & Rockliff, 1961), J. P. T. Bury, *Napoleon* III *and the Second Empire* (English Universities Press, 1964) and Jasper Ridley, *Napoleon* III *and Eugénie* (Constable, 1979). Studies on particular aspects of the Second Empire include L. M. Case, *French Opinion on War and Diplomacy during the Second Empire* (University of Pennsylvania Press, 1954), Theodore Zeldin, *The Political System of Napoleon* III (Macmillan 1958) and *Emile Ollivier and the Liberal Empire of Napoleon* III (Oxford University Press, 1963), D. H. Pinkney, *Napoleon* III *and the Rebuilding of Paris* (Princeton University Press, 1958) and Roger L. Williams, *The Mortal Napoleon* (Princeton University Press, 1971). The last mentioned deals with the effect that the emperor's state of health had on his government of France. See also chapter 19 of Theodore Zeldin, *France 1848–1945*, vol I (Oxford University Press 1973), and for documents on the Second Empire see David Thomson (ed.), *France: Empire and Republic 1850–1940* (Harper & Row, 1968) and Alison Patrick (ed.), *The Empire of the Third Napoleon* (Edward Arnold, 1973). Alfred Cobban, *A History of Modern France*, vol II (Penguin, 1961) usefully summarises in his narrative the findings of some of the specialist studies mentioned above.

1 Duc Albert de Broglie (1821–1901) reflects in his Memoirs on Louis Napoleon's Seizure of Power

I have told by what mixture of good and bad reasons the leaders of the conservative party in the Constituent Assembly persuaded us to give our votes for the Presidency of the Republic to the nephew and heir of the first Emperor. . . . I do not think that any of us doubted that he would try

5 to become Emperor, least of all would I insult M. Thiers, who had advised us to support him, by implying that he had not anticipated such a natural eventuality. He simply thought, and we thought the same, that once we had made use of the popularity of his name to overthrow the revolutionary usurpers of February 1848 and restabilize the bases of a 10 disturbed society, we should retain the influence to prevent him whenever he tried to transform the power which had been entrusted to him for the public weal into an instrument of personal aggrandisement. . . .

It is probable that it would have been a very simple matter if the 15 President Prince had been such as his exploits at Boulogne and Strasbourg had led us to suppose, and such as he had been judged by those of our leaders who had known him on the benches of the Constituent Assembly, an adventurer who was both mad and incapable, with the confidence of a visionary in his imperial star, but lacking experience, knowledge or 20 reliable resources of character and intelligence. Such a man who had been put to the test for three years, and submitted to the flood of light on his power which so few reputations and popular figures survive, would have been rapidly discredited. . . .

Far from being diminished and weakened during his three years' 25 Presidency, on the contrary the Prince had increased the public's esteem and confidence in him; and it was becoming much more difficult to bring him down from power than if we had tried to prevent his attaining it. There were now added, to the blind votes of the crowd who had placed him over us, the support of all the commercial and industrial interests 30 which had been thrown into confusion by the February crisis, and which could breathe again since he had taken the reins of government. What qualities did he possess which enabled him to achieve the very rare distinction of being still more popular after his trial period than beforehand? It was somewhat difficult to say, and our friends in 35 particular, knowing that he was devoid of those talents which had made the fortune of public men under the parliamentary regime – eloquence, administrative ability, wide knowledge and a cultivated mind – were at a loss to understand. He had qualities of a different order, patient skill, the art of not compromising himself between the different parties which a 40 fortuitous coalition had grouped round him, the ability to dissimulate his thoughts, and when on rare occasions he decided to speak in public, the gift of finding the right word which reflected general opinion.

David Thomson (ed.), *France: Empire and Republic 1850–1940*, 1968, pp 37–8

Questions

* *a* Explain the following: (i) Louis Napoleon's 'exploits at Boulogne and Strasbourg' (line 15); (ii) the significance of February 1848 (lines 9 and 30).

* *b* Outline the career of M. Thiers (line 5) up to the end of 1848.
c Why did French politicians such as the Duc de Broglie support Louis Napoleon's candidature for the presidency of France in 1848?
d Why did the Broglie's expectations about Louis Napoleon prove to be incorrect?
* *e* '[T]he different parties which a fortuitous coalition had grouped round him' (lines 39–40). To which sections of French society did Louis Napoleon's actions as president appeal?
* *f* Why was the Second Republic so short-lived?

2 The Napoleonic Idea, 1852 and 1870

(a) On October 9, 1852, at a banquet given by the Chamber of Commerce at Bordeaux, Louis Bonaparte proclaimed the Empire, adding the significant words, '*L'Empire c'est la Paix*'. The French nation, being consulted for the third time, for the third time by an overwhelming
5 majority ratified its belief in Bonapartism. On December 1, 1852, the Prince President was proclaimed Emperor under the title Napoleon III.

The programme of the Empire was not the improvisation of a vulgar adventurer, but the result of long reflection on the Napoleonic tradition and on the best means of adapting it to the needs of France. 'The name
10 Napoleon,' so ran the message of October 31, 1849, 'is a complete programme in itself; it stands for order, authority, religion, the welfare of the people within; without, for national dignity.' Napoleon professed himself to be the elect of the people, and ready to abandon his prerogatives at their desire. It was necessary that he should begin his
15 career as Emperor by depriving the country of that exercise of political liberty which in his judgement had been so fatal to France ever since the battle of Waterloo; but by degrees he would limit his prerogatives and admit the nation to a share in government. Like his uncle, he had come not to suppress but to adjourn the reign of political freedom and to
20 educate the French people in the art of combining self-government, progress, and order.

The Napoleonic idea, as he had already explained, stood not for war but for peace. 'I have,' he said at Bordeaux, October 9, 1852, 'like the Emperor, conquests to make. Like him, I wish to draw into the stream of
25 the great popular river those hostile side-currents which tend to lose themselves without profit to any one. . . . I wish to conquer for religion, morality, and prosperity, that part of the population, still so numerous, which in the midst of a country of faith and belief scarcely knows the precept of Christ, which in the heart of the most fertile country in the
30 world can scarcely enjoy the prime necessities of its produce. We have immense districts of virgin soil to clear, roads to open, harbours to dig, rivers to render navigable, canals to finish, our network of railways to complete. Opposite to Marseilles there is a vast kingdom waiting to be

assimilated to France. Our great ports of the West must be brought near
35 to the American continent by the rapidity of the commerce we have yet to create. We have everywhere ruins to restore, false gods to overthrow, truths to establish in triumph. That is how I should understand the Empire, if the Empire is to be re-established.'

(b) Seven million votes testified the assent of France to the Liberal
40 Empire, and there are some who still believe that, but for the momentary aberration of judgement which led to the Franco-Prussian war, the principle of Liberalism might have saved the Empire of Napoleon. There is some reason to question this decision. A government is only strong if it adheres to its guiding principle. The guiding principle of Bonapartism
45 was autocracy founded on popular consent, safeguarding social order and equality. An autocrat does not easily abdicate to a parliamentary ministry, does not easily adapt himself to the delicate mechanism of constitutional forms. And in France, though there was still no little personal attachment to Napoleon, faith in the Empire had declined. Who
50 could be enthusiastic for a government with such a record of humiliation and failure? Could the Liberals forgive the harsh tyranny of the earlier years? Could they trust a nephew of Napoleon to unlearn the traditions of his house? . . . In our view Bonapartism was a spent force before Count Bismarck changed the Ems telegram.

H. A. L. Fisher, *Bonapartism*, 1908, pp 143–5, 198–201

Questions

a Explain the following: (i) 'being consulted for the third time' (line 4); (ii) 'a vast kingdom' (line 33); (iii) 'the Liberal Empire' (lines 39–40); (iv) 'the Ems telegram' (line 54).

* *b* How had the 'Napoleonic tradition' (line 8) taken shape in France between 1815 and 1848?

c According to these extracts, how does Louis Napoleon interpret the idea of 'Bonapartism'?

* *d* Did Napoleon III pursue the policies outlined here in his conduct of France's foreign and domestic affairs or does the evidence suggest that these utterances were simply 'window-dressing'?

e What aspect of the political programme set out by Louis Napoleon does H. A. L. Fisher suggest was unworkable?

3 Napoleon III: the 'Arriviste who Arrived'

It was the tragedy of Napoleon III that he did not die until twenty years after his life had lost its purpose. He had lived, since he came of age, by the

light of a single star which shone above the Tuileries and would make him, as he believed, Emperor of the French . . . and at forty-five, a pallid
5 man with dull eyes, he was the Emperor of the French and the husband of a beautiful woman. But the star flickered and failed, since on attaining his purpose he had lost it: it was the tragedy of an *arriviste* who arrived.

In his odd, silent way, behind the dull mask and the great moustache, the man had known he would be king. . . . But he knew nothing more
10 about the future. It was written, of course; and a wise man would watch the slow drift of events without thrusting rashly across the stream. His attitude was always that of a man who, in his own phrase, '*attend un évenement*'. 'I never form distant plans,' he once told a king's secretary, 'I am governed by the exigencies of the moment.' . . . The world thought
15 him designing. . . . Palmerston warned Gladstone that he was 'an able, active, wary, counsel-keeping but ever-planning sovereign.' . . . But he made few plans; he was indifferent to the choice of men to act for him, because he believed that without plans or men that which was written would come to pass. . . . So it was that for twenty years he seemed to
20 drift, since it was useless to strive against the stream; a sphinx, since he answered no questions; an enigma to the world, since his own intentions were an enigma to himself.

He had been a man of one idea; and when it was accomplished, he was left without one. . . . Yet there was one further principle which seemed
25 to gleam vaguely through all his opportunism. He still believed, as he had written in 1839, that the world should be made up of free nations, and he was haunted through his policy by a half-formed idea (had he not trained Italian guns against the *Papalini* in 1831?) that Italy must be freed by a Bonaparte.

Philip Guedalla, *The Second Empire*, 1932, pp 190–2

Questions

a What is meant by an '*arriviste*' (line 7)?

* *b* Explain the reference to Louis Napoleon's actions in 1831.

c What is the main target of Philip Guedalla's critical assessment of Napoleon III?

d Do you find the way in which Philip Guedalla has presented his argument convincing? Do you think he may have been influenced in his assessment of Napoleon III by his personal feelings about events and personalities of his own day?

* *e* What explanation does Guedalla suggest for Napoleon III's intervention in Italian affairs? Could less 'romantic' motives be ascribed to the emperor?

f Compare the impressions of Napoleon III given by the extracts from Fisher and Guedalla. Which do you think gives a fairer view of the part 'principles' played in his conduct of French government?

4 Theodore Zeldin on Napoleon III as a Subject for Biography

(a) Napoleon III, as emperor, did not possess the power to do as he pleased. He inherited institutions, customs and legal practices from his predecessors, so that his was a modified rather than a completely reshaped version of previous governments. The three major constitutional changes
5 were the reduced independence of ministers, the diminished powers of parliament and the increased vigour in censoring and suppressing opposition. But Napoleon had to act through individuals of widely different backgrounds and ideas. . . . In 1852 Napoleon may have appeared to be the absolute master of France but the history of his reign
10 cannot be summarised in his own biography. Certainly, he determined personally the general direction of government policy but he was not sufficiently assiduous in administration nor sufficiently attentive to detail to get his will regularly enforced in practice.

Theodore Zeldin, *France 1848–1945*, 1973, vol I, pp. 513–4

15 (b) Napoleon's guiding principle was that you must keep up with the times. For him, that meant, to a large extent, following the lead of England, where he was almost as much at home as in France. But though he admired private enterprise as the key to English success, he had reservations about its results: he feared large cities and dreamed of
20 enticing the urban masses back to the land. His misfortune was that England did not admire him in return and was always suspicious of his ambitions: no one ever knew what he would do next. He loved scheming to put the world to rights.

A monarch's reputation depends in part on the way he treats
25 intellectuals. It is they who write history, and they do not forgive easily. It took at least half a century before they were willing to acknowledge that Napoleon had claims to being considered an astute politician, even if he did persecute them. He survived on the throne so long because he offered some advantages to almost every class, though not necessarily to the
30 whole of every class. Like the Shah of Iran he made the mistake of alienating the Church; but unlike him, he saw the need to win over the liberal opposition; his concessions to it (or rather to part of it, for he knew how to divide his enemies) almost worked. Had he not messed up his relations with Germany, he might have established a dynasty.

35 Napoleon III has attracted many biographers, but he has always eluded them. He was too secretive, too devious, too silent – a conspirator even when in power – to leave enough records for a full portrait of him to be possible. The best biographies of him stop in mid-career: once he became emperor, his personal life becomes more enigmatic than ever. . . .

40 Napoleon III is probably not a man to approach through biography. To judge him, one must make up one's mind not only about his character, but even more about what he did to his country. Historians are increasingly rejecting the view that he was as omnipotent a ruler as his

contemporaries believed; the transformations of his reign cannot be
45 ascribed precisely to his influence. His advisers and his civil servants had a great deal of independence, and often moved in contradictory directions; the masses did not obey them blindly, and were not simply pushed around.

Theodore Zeldin in the *Observer*, 25 November 1979, reviewing Jasper Ridley, *Napoleon* III *and Eugénie*

[In his foreword, Jasper Ridley writes, 'This is not a history of the Second Empire but a biography of Louis Napoleon and a biography of Eugénie.']

Questions

a What factors prevented Napoleon III from being the 'absolute master' of France (line 9)?

* *b* In what ways did Napoleon III alienate the church in France (line 31)?

c In what respects is Zeldin's verdict on Napoleon III more favourable than that of Guedalla?

* *d* '(T)he transformations of his reign cannot be ascribed precisely to his influence' (lines 44–5). In what ways was France in 1870 different from France in 1852? How would you assess the relationship between these changes and Napoleon III's policies?

e What does Theodore Zeldin see as the limitations of biographies of Napoleon III?

5 The End of the Empire

After its Crimean and Italian triumphs, the government might be allowed an unlucky foray in Mexico, but the rise of Prussia on the northern horizon, the defeat of Austria, and French isolation caused dismay. Napoleon gave a bellicose speech to test public opinion and
5 discovered that France was not willing to fight for territorial compensations. Then, when it was too late, the secret reports showed that all but four departments were for war. 'Everybody says,' observed a minister, summarising the situation, 'that greatness is a relative thing, and that a country can be reduced while remaining the same, when new forces
10 increase around it.' The Empress foresaw 'the beginning of the end of the dynasty'. Yet when an attempt was made to strengthen the army the prefects reported a general unwillingness. . . . At first, France had wanted both peace and glory, and Napoleon in his prime had kept the balance. Now, it was peace and security that were desired, and an ageing
15 ruler failed to convince the country that a price must be paid to make the two compatible.

Constitutional concessions ought to have been made in the days of

glory. Now they came under the shadow of decline. In January 1867, the *Moniteur* announced a liberalization of the regime. 'Interpellations'
20 would be allowed in parliament and laws would be proposed to free the press. But the Emperor was haunted by the reactionaries, particularly Rouher and the Empress, prophesying doom; he was ill, suffering agonies from the stone; he was unwilling to make his concessions appear like 'asking pardon for Mexico and Germany'. . . . In the elections of 1869,
25 the government vote was down by more than a million, and the Bonapartist 'Third Party' led the way in asking for responsibility of ministers. On 8 September this was granted, together with other constitutional reforms. The Emperor was known to be acting unwillingly.

30 Yet the point of decisive change had been reached, and on the eve of its downfall the Empire achieved a form in which it might have endured. . . . The constitution of April 1870 made France into a parliamentary regime and in May, a plebiscite gave approval with over 7,350,000 affirmative votes. Napoleon was happy. '*J'ai mon chiffre*' – he
35 had roughly the same number of votes as he had collected after the *coup d'état*. A parliament with new powers met on 18 May: the Empire then had three months to go.

It could have endured. War, and not the logic of internal developments ended it. . . . The Empire had been feared in the world as a military
40 regime and Frenchmen were confident in its arms: in fact, out of deference to public opinion, Napoleon had economized on the army and defeat was certain.

J. McManners, *Lectures on European History 1789–1914*, 1966, pp. 229–31

Questions

a Explain the following: (i) 'Interpellations' (line 19); (ii) '*J'ai mon chiffre*' (lines 34–5).

b Explain the meaning of lines 14–6.

c Is it justifiable to describe Napoleon III's involvement in the Crimean war and Italian affairs as 'triumphs' (line 1)?

* *d* Why did France become involved in an 'unlucky foray in Mexico' (line 2) and what was the outcome?

* *e* What kind of 'territorial compensations' (lines 5–6) did Napoleon III attempt to obtain for France to offset the rise of Prussia? Why was he unsuccessful?

f How did Napoleon III seek to establish what 'public opinion' was on a particular issue? How does the period leading up to the Franco-Prussian war bring out the dangers for a country of having a government which feels dependent on public opinion?

g Compare the views of Guedalla, Zeldin and McManners on the prospects for the continuance of the empire in 1870. What evidence can be used to support the different viewpoints?

6 Napoleon III: 'the first Mountebank Dictator'

Napoleon III and Boulanger were to be the plagiarists, shadowy and counterfeit, of Napoleon I; and Mussolini and Hitler were to be unconscious reproducers of the methods of Napoleon III. For these are inherent in plebiscitarian Caesarism, or so-called 'Caesarian democracy', 5 with its direct appeal to the masses: demagogical slogans; disregard of legality in spite of a professed guardianship of law and order; contempt of political parties and the parliamentary system, of the educated classes and their values; blandishments and vague, contradictory promises for all and sundry; militarism; gigantic, blatant displays and shady corruption. 10 *Panem et circenses* once more – and at the end of the road, disaster. . . .

The careers of Napoleon III and Hitler have shown how far even a bare minimum of ideas and resources, when backed by a nation's reminiscences or passions, can carry a man in the political desert of 'direct democracy'; and the books written about Napoleon III show how loath 15 posterity is to accept the stark truth about such a man. And yet a careful examination of the evidence merely confirms the opinion of leading contemporaries about him: the enigma was not so much in him as in the disparity between his own spiritual stature and the weight of the ideas centred on him. Dream pictures are best projected on to a blank screen – 20 which, however, neither fixes nor brings them to life.

How much can be safely said of Napoleon III? Biographers agree that there was something in him which defies definition and description: obviously the unstable, the shapeless, the void cannot be delineated. He was reticent, secretive, conspiratorial; at times his power of silence created 25 the appearance of strength. Narrow and rigid in his ideas, out of touch with reality, he was a dreamer entertaining vast, nebulous schemes, but vacillating, confused, and therefore complex and ineffective in action. . . . He talked high and vague idealism, uncorrelated to his actions. He had a fixed, superstitious, childish belief in his name and star. 30 Risen to power, this immature weak man became a public danger. His silence was self-defence: to cover up his inadequacy and to preserve him from the impact of stronger personalities, of demands which he would have found difficult to resist, of arguments to which he had no reply; it also helped him to avoid commitments. . . . He would bide his time – 35 which with him meant inactive waiting without any approach to reality. He tumbled into situations, neither designed nor deliberately created by him. When forced to act, the day-dreamer would try to draw back: so it was before the *coup d'état*, and again in 1859 – in fact in almost every crisis. But if the initiative had passed out of his hands he would drift 40 anxiety-ridden, fumbling, wishing to call a halt, and mostly unable to do so. Under stress his personality seemed to disintegrate.

Sir Lewis Namier, *Vanished Supremacies: Essays on European History 1812–1918*, 1958, pp 54–63.

[The essay from which this extract comes, 'The First Mountebank Dictator', was first published in 1947 and is essentially an extended review of Albert Guérard, *Napoleon III*, 1943, which takes a favourable view of the emperor.]

Questions

a Explain the following: (i) 'plagiarists' (line 1); (ii) 'plebiscitarian Caesarism' (line 4); (iii) 'demagogical slogans' (line 5); (iv) '*Panem et circenses*' (line 10).

b Why does Namier call Napoleon III a 'mountebank dictator'?

* *c* Explain how the phrase 'backed by a nation's reminiscences or passions' could apply to Napoleon III's France and to Hitler's Germany.

* *d* What similarities does Namier see between the regimes of Napoleon III and Mussolini and Hitler? Do you think that the differences are more significant than the similarities?

e Compare Namier's highly critical view of Napoleon's character and political system with that of McManners and Zeldin. Do Namier's views coincide with those of Guedalla at all?

Further Work

a 'For Louis Napoleon, Bonapartism was no more than a propaganda device for making himself Emperor.' Is the meaning of Bonapartism irrelevant to the study of the Second Empire?

b Zeldin expresses the view that Napoleon's 'guiding principle was that you must keep up with the times', whereas Namier believes that he was 'out of touch with reality'. How successful was Napoleon III in taking account of the changing French and European scene during the Second Empire?

c 'Biography can almost be described as an endangered species in terms of serious historical scholarship.' Why should this be so; why do new biographies of men such as Napoleon III continue to appear; and do biographies still have an important part to play in our understanding of the past?

VI International Socialism and the Paris Commune, 1871

Introduction

This section deals with interpretations of an episode which was both an important event in French history and also a landmark in the development of international socialism in the nineteenth century. The extracts show how careful the historian has to be in making generalisations and applying labels, particularly ideological ones, when discussing the motives and beliefs of a group of individuals, such as the population of Paris in 1871. The chief problems which need to be considered in assessing the significance of the Commune are these: how far social discontent and socialist ideas helped to bring about the uprising; how far the Commune was a government of working-class people, acting in the interest of the working classes, during the seventy-two days in which it ruled Paris; and how we should define the terms 'socialist' and 'working class' in relation to Paris at this time. The views of three historians on how these problems should be approached are given in the extracts below.

As the first extract in this section shows, those who lived through the Commune found it hard to understand what was happening around them. The name Commune was itself misleading, since it seemed to identify the uprising with the philosophy of 'communism'. In reality, it looked back to the days of the French Revolution and the Commune of 1793, and beyond that to the independent cities of the middle ages. For propaganda purposes, both critics and supporters of the Commune in 1871 chose to label it as a movement which aimed to overturn the existing social order. When Bismark expressed the view that Paris seemed simply to be seeking a greater degree of municipal self-government, the socialist deputy, August Bebel, declared in the Reichstag, 'If the Paris Commune fought only for communal liberties, all the gunpowder fired would have been in vain.'

This view is echoed in the final extract by Eugene Schulkind. Nevertheless, the only official programme of the Commune, published on 19 April 1871, certainly had as its keynote the aim of reorganising France as a federation of equal and self-governing communes. This represented the policy of one faction in the First International Working Men's Association, formed in 1864, namely the followers of Joseph-

Pierre Proudhon. It was very different from Karl Marx's idea of achieving a new society through the dictatorship of the proletariat. The failure of the Commune helped to discredit Proudhon's federalist ideas, and by the time the Second International was formed in 1889, Marx's brand of socialism had become predominant.

In an influential piece of 'contemporary history', Marx had seized the opportunity to produce an analysis of the Commune in 1871 in line with his own political ideas, an extract from which is included below. In the bitter aftermath of the Commune, Marx stressed the moderation of the communards, but nevertheless he proclaimed that whatever their motives or actions, the fact that 'plain working men' had seized and exercised power for the first time, made it the 'glorious harbinger of a new society'. Marx himself was well aware that the argument could not be pressed too far. As he wrote to a colleague in 1881, 'The Commune was merely the rising of a town under exceptional conditions; the majority of the Commune was in no sense socialist, nor could it be. With a small amount of common sense, they could have reached a compromise with Versailles useful to the whole mass of the people.' But there was no compromise, and the ferocity with which the Commune was suppressed in May 1871 seemed ample justification for Marx's view of the inevitability of class warfare and provided the socialist movement with its indispensable martyrs.

Further Reading

For the military events leading up to the Paris Commune, see Michael Howard, *The Franco-Prussian War* (Hart-Davis, 1961) and Alistair Horne, *The Fall of Paris* (Macmillan, 1965); and for background on the ideas of the left in France, see John Plamenatz, *The Revolutionary Movement in France 1815–71* (Longmans, Green, 1952), John McManners, *Lectures on European History 1789–1914*, chapter 20 (Blackwell, 1966) and Theodore Zeldin, *France 1848–1945*, vol I, chapter 23 (Oxford University Press, 1973). Further collections of documents can be found in Eugene Schulkind, *The Paris Commune of 1871: the View from the Left* (Cape, 1972) and Stewart Edwards, *The Communards of Paris* (Thames & Hudson, 1973). The former has also produced the Historical Association pamphlet, *The Paris Commune of 1871* (Pamphlet 78, 1971) and the latter has published a history of the Commune, *The Paris Commune* (Eyre & Spottiswoode, 1971). A valuable history of the Commune by one who took part in it is Prosper-Oliver Lissagaray, *History of the Paris Commune of 1871* (1876, reprinted by New Park Publications, 1976). The different ways in which the Commune has been interpreted are covered by E. Mason, *The Paris Commune* (Macmillan, 1930) and J. Roberts, 'The Myth of the Commune' in *History Today*, May 1957. Roger L. Williams, *The French Revolution of 1870–1* (Norton, 1969) puts the Commune into the context of the transition from the Second Empire to the Third Republic.

1 An Anonymous Parisian reports on the Commune

Paris, 24 March 1871: What has been long feared by honest men of all parties has been at last brought about. . . . There is a strange unanimity in denouncing the Parisian insurgents as the paid tools of the hated Bismarck. The idea is that the Prussians wished to provoke some armed 5 opposition to their entry of the city on the 1st of this month, as an excuse for organised pillage, and that, when this design failed, from the admirable self-command of the great body of our people, they opened a communication with some of the reddest of the Reds. . . .

Paris, 24 April 1871: We have now had more than a month of 10 Communistic no-government administered by men of whose very names few ever heard before. Yet in truth we cannot say that our very natural apprehensions when we found ourselves in their hands have been realised. The object that they profess to aim at, namely, a sort of Federation of Paris and other cities, each sovereign and irresponsible, of 15 course would be the utter ruin of the country could it be carried out, and it would be a less evil to be partitioned by our open enemies at once. But though things now look very dark, neither of these matters will come to pass, I feel assured. . . .

Paris, 20 May 1871: The suicidal civil war between the Commune and the 20 Assembly whatever it may have been in the beginning, is evidently now nothing more than a contest between Monarchy and ultra-Republicanism. In the Assembly, as in the country, Monarchists of some shade or other (and including Imperialists), are in a vast majority; but it is usually the active minority that really direct affairs all over the world, and 25 when they have a gleam of success, the sluggish majority join itself to them. So it is here in Paris. . . .

Unhappily there is the disturbing element of the 'International Association', which some people begin to think the main cause of our present troubles. Certain it is, that a motley collection of foreigners are 30 enrolled in the army of the Commune, though whether they are quite as numerous as *Le Gaulois* asserted a few days ago, I am not prepared to say. . . .

At the present date we are governed in Paris by a variety of bodies – more, in fact, than I can undertake to enumerate. However, that does not 35 much matter, as they all seem to be controlled by a body of five citizens, newly formed, with the ominous title of the Committee of Public Safety. Except the extravagance of decreeing the destruction of the Colonne Vendôme (since carried into effect) as 'an offence to the fraternity of nations' – a proceeding in which the hand of the International Associ-40 ation is seen – the Commune really has kept far more within the bounds of moderation than there seemed any reason to expect. It is not true that there was any general pillage of the churches, or more arbitrary interference by private individuals than the Empire long practised with impunity. But I fear things are on the change for the worse under the 45 dictatorship of the Committee. . . . Generals are made and unmade at their pleasure. . .; a commission appointed to select subjects for retaliation for cruelties ascribed to the Versailles troops. . .; churches turned by order into debating clubs, and their property actually seized – the Commune only threatened this.

50 *Paris, 24 June 1871*: The Commune has at last been hurled down. In its brief existence it has done a world of mischief, and it has sown the seeds of more. . . .

Royal United Service Magazine 1871, part I, pp 575–6; part II, pp 93, 260–3, 421

Questions

a On 24 March 1871 what events had just taken place in Paris which had 'been long feared by honest men' (line 1)?

b How do the writer's views concerning the Commune – its conduct and aims – change between 24 March and 24 June 1871? From which social and political class do you think the anonymous reporter came?

c What is meant by the 'Assembly' (line 22)? Why were the 'conservative' elements in a majority?

* *d* What is meant by the 'International Association' (lines 27–8)? How important a part did it play in the Commune?

e Why should the name 'Committee of Public Safety' be regarded as 'ominous'? (line 36)

f Explain why the Colonne Vendôme was regarded as 'an offence to the fraternity of nations' (lines 37–8)?

2 Karl Marx's View of the Commune

[*Napoleon III has been defeated and the Republic has been proclaimed.*]

Paris, however, was not to be defended without arming its working class, organising them into an effective force, and training their ranks by the war itself. But Paris armed was the Revolution armed. A victory of Paris over the Prussian aggressor would have been a victory of the French
5 workman over the French capitalist and his State parasites. In this conflict between national duty and class interest, the Government of National Defence did not hesitate one moment to turn into a Government of National Defection. . . .

It was only by the violent overthrow of the Republic that the
10 appropriators of wealth could hope to shift on to the shoulders of its producers the cost of the war which they, the appropriators, had themselves originated. Thus, the immense ruin of France spurred on these patriotic representatives of land and capital, under the very eyes and patronage of the invader to graft upon the foreign war a civil war – a
15 slaveholders' rebellion. Armed Paris was the only serious obstacle in the way of counter-revolutionary conspiracy. . . . Still, in its abhorrence of

the civil war into which Paris was to be goaded, the Central Committee continued to persist in a merely defensive attitude, despite the provocations of the Assembly. . . . Thiers opened the civil war by sending Vinoy . . . upon a nocturnal expedition against Montmartre, there to seize, by surprise, the artillery of the National Guard. . . . The glorious working men's Revolution of the 18th March took undisputed sway of Paris. . . .

The multiplicity of interpretations to which the Commune has been subjected, and the multiplicity of interests which construed it in their favour, show that it was a thoroughly expansive political form, while all previous forms of government had been emphatically repressive. Its true secret was this. It was essentially a working-class government, the produce of the struggle of the producing against the appropriating class, the political form at last discovered under which to work out the economical emancipation of Labour. . . .

When the Paris Commune took the management of the revolution in its own hands; when plain working men for the first time dared to infringe upon the Governmental privilege of their 'natural superiors', and, under circumstances of unexampled difficulty, performed their work modestly, conscientiously, and efficiently . . . the old world writhed in convulsions of rage at the sight of the Red Flag, the symbol of the Republic of Labour, floating over the Hotel de Ville. . . . The great social measure of the Commune was its own working existence. . . .

The conspiracy of the ruling class to break down the Revolution by a civil war carried on under the patronage of the foreign invader . . . culminated in the carnage of Paris. . . . Class rule is no longer able to disguise itself in a national uniform; the national governments are one as against the proletariate! After Whit-Sunday 1871, there can be neither peace nor truce possible between the working men of France and the appropriators of their produce. . . .

Working men's Paris, with its Commune, will be for ever celebrated as the glorious harbinger of a new society. Its martyrs are enshrined in the great heart of the working class. Its exterminators' history has already been nailed to that eternal pillory from which all the prayers of their priest will not avail to redeem them.

Karl Marx, *The Civil War in France*, an address delivered to the General Council of the International Working Men's Association on 30 May 1871, in David Fernbach (ed.), *Karl Marx: The First International and After: Political Writings*, 1974, vol III, pp 187–233

Questions

a What is meant by the following: (i) 'State parasites' (line 5); (ii) 'a slaveholders' rebellion' (line 15) (iii) 'the Central Committee' (line 17); (iv) 'After Whit-Sunday 1871' (line 44)?

b According to Marx, who was responsible for the civil war and what were their motives? Is there any evidence to support his charges?

* *c* What acts by the National Assembly could be regarded as 'provocations' (line 19) towards Paris?

* *d* Is Marx justified in saying that the Commune behaved 'modestly, conscientiously and efficiently' (line 36)?

e Explain carefully what claims Marx makes for the 'revolutionary' significance of the Commune. In what way does he see it as 'the glorious harbinger of a new society' (line 48)?

3 The Leadership of the Commune Analysed

[The Commune] was first of all not the result of any revolution. Two attempts to start an insurrection by the revolutionaries in the city – chiefly Blanquists – on 31 October 1870 and 22 January 1871, were complete fiascos, raising virtually no support. . . . It was not an upsurge
5 of socialism or any new force that produced the Commune. Paris did not rebel. Rather the Commune was brought about by the conservatives wishing to end the old problem of Parisian insubordination. Thiers had an old score to settle with the city which had overthrown him in 1848. . . . It was this withdrawal of the government that created the
10 Commune and made Paris autonomous for 73 days. . . .

As a result – and this is perhaps what makes the Commune so fascinating and important to the historian – it is possible now to see Paris naked, for its conventional clothes were suddenly removed. One can see just where the government and the economic system were repressive –
15 where the clothes had been too tight – but also where masses would continue to behave as they had always done even when official obligations and sanctions were withdrawn. . . .

The first thing Paris did on finding itself independent was to hold elections for a municipal council – which then assumed the name of
20 Commune. Twenty-five manual workers (artisans) were returned, and this gave the Commune a uniquely proletarian flavour – but the sixty-five other members were bourgeois – doctors, teachers, lawyers, journalists. About one-third of the population of Paris had left during the war or after the siege, including most of the upper classes: the leadership
25 of the city significantly devolved to the petty bourgeoisie, when the top layer – social and governmental – were removed. Two-thirds of these ninety members of the Commune were Jacobins, inspired not by a vision of a socialist future, but by memories of the Revolution of 1789, seeing the Commune as a continuation of that of 1793, capturing power in the
30 interests of the people and using the authority of the state to destroy its enemies. Only one-third were in some way socialists and these were divided between Proudhonists, seeking the abolition of the state, and Blanquist revolutionaries. The acts of the Commune were generally the work of the Jacobins, but the manifestos and justifications of these actions

35 were written by the theoretical Proudhonists. So the aims of the Commune are, not surprisingly, difficult to discover, and all the more so because even this division between Jacobins, Proudhonists and Blanquists is too simple. The Jacobins were not necessarily anti-socialist for some were members of the International. Most social reforms were voted
40 unanimously. The Blanquists had much in common with the Jacobins. There was no coherent socialist minority group, which only existed, if at all, at the very end of the Commune, when they had got to know each other. In any case very few acted consistently according to any one doctrine. . . .

45 The Commune's main preoccupation was to feed and defend itself against the government of Versailles. It had no time to institute, let alone to try out, any far-reaching reforms. The atmosphere of war and siege was not conducive to careful planning. . . .

Theodore Zeldin, *France 1848–1945*, 1973, vol I, pp 736–40

Questions

* *a* What were the circumstances of the risings on 31 October 1870 and 22 January 1871? Why were they 'complete fiascos' (line 4)?

b Who, according to Theodore Zeldin, was responsible for the civil war? Compare his view with Marx's.

* *c* Describe the origins and ideas of the different groups referred to in this extract: (i) Socialists; (ii) Jacobins; (iii) Blanquists; (iv) Proudhonists.

d How does Theodore Zeldin show that ideological labels must be used with caution in analysing the acts of the Commune?

e How far does Theodore Zeldin's analysis support Karl Marx's view that it was 'essentially a working-class government' (extract 2, line 28)?

f What does Theodore Zeldin see as the special value for the historian in studying the Paris Commune? What conclusions can one draw from the fact that the Commune did not overturn the economic and social order in Paris?

4 The 'Rank and File' of the Commune

(a) The impression one gains from the interrogation of prisoners is one of men bewildered by events, in which they have somehow been caught up for reasons which they cannot explain. Most blamed their participation on their dependence on the pay they received as National Guards. One
5 Léopold Caucheteux, a mason, replied when asked if he had recognised the Commune as a legal government that 'No, I recognised it because it gave me 2 francs 50 centimes a day, and 0 francs 75 centimes to my wife, with which I could feed my children. '. . . Similarly a clerk, accused of usurpation of public functions in that he continued to work in his office

10 after the establishment of the Commune, blamed this on the necessity of
earning a living.

Another very common reason given was the pressure from friends and
neighbours – thus François Godin, a 51-year-old fruit merchant, com-
plained that 'Pressed from all sides by neighbours and friends with whom
15 I had served during the siege, I did not dare refuse; they always came to
find me. . . .' Inertia was an element in this; a clerk called Hippolyte
Bisson admitted remaining with the 33rd battalion of the National Guard
during the Commune: 'I belonged to this battalion during the war against
the Prussians, and as it continued to exist during the Commune I believed
20 it was my duty to remain with it. . . .' Fear was another aspect –
Hippolyte Fretel, a bronze worker, excused himself: 'I was forced to
march by the threats of the others, and from fear of the Commune's
courts martial.' Many men claimed to have served only reluctantly and
from fear because, as the mason Florent Bartholemy claimed, 'They came
25 to look for me at work and I had to march or be shot.'

Many claimed to have been concerned solely to defend order in their
own quarters, but in spite of the obvious unwillingness of most to admit
to a deliberate decision to fight for the Commune some were more honest
or foolhardy. At their simplest the reasons given are typified by the reply
30 of one Alfred Cavala, a domestic, when asked what the Commune meant
for him: 'Everyone would be free.' Better-educated prisoners claimed to
have been defending republican institutions or indeed municipal liberties.
Some were openly self-seeking – one wine-merchant admitted to
serving the Commune in the hope of protecting his business, and a lawyer
35 who had acted as delegate of the Commune at the town hall of the 9th
arrondissement, claimed to have done so 'to acquire a reputation in the
quarter so as to be able later to increase my clientele'. More typically, a
cabinet-maker accused of having said that he would pay his proprietor
with a bullet admitted that he had been worried about how to pay his
40 rent.

Of great significance was the fact that a number of witnesses
maintained that the role of women was important in encouraging their
menfolk. The military authorities prepared a special report on the
participation of women, claiming that most had believed a new era was
45 about to begin. For the men who fought and the women who
encouraged them the Commune meant immediately a wage, and
eventually a new society in which the poverty and insecurity, experienced above all by women attempting to cook for and clothe their
families, would no longer exist. It was for material improvement and
50 human dignity that men fought – their reluctance in most stages of the
Commune indicates perhaps their limited faith in the vague promises of
their leaders, but also the failure of these to develop an appealing ideology
and the inevitably even more limited political and social consciousness of
the led. In this respect little progress had been made since 1848. It was
55 only in the last days when, with the army inside Paris, they were
defending their own quarters and their homes that for many Com-

munards the struggle came alive and had meaning. Henry Maret wrote of the butchery of these days that 'The massacre was not only a crime; it was for the reaction itself a grievous fault. The Commune, which would have faded out in ridicule, assumed a tragic grandeur.'

The last desperate struggle and the butchery with which it was ended created heroes and martyrs for the socialist movement to glorify. Conservatives looked on the Commune as a rising of the depraved and criminal, a new eruption of barbarism. Two polarised conceptions emerged and, as society grew more humane, or socialism more tamed and respectable, the heroic picture became dominant. The whole episode was one which attracted left-wing intellectuals who were historians, and the evidence they used was mainly composed of the speeches and writings of other intellectuals who had participated in the Commune. We must not exaggerate the degree to which simplification occurred, but simplification there was. . . .

To the heroic picture in which the workers storm the heights of the old corrupt society to create a new world must be added darker tints. When the expressed motives of the rank and file are considered, it was not conscious creation which seems to have been dominant but the desire to escape the brutalities of harsh everyday existence. Motivation was not ideological but practical. . . . Wherever possible the common man must be allowed to speak for himself rather than have motives ascribed to him by intellectual observers or those engaged in police work.

R. D. Price, 'Ideology and Motivation in the Paris Commune of 1871', in *The Historical Journal*, 1972, pp 84–6

(b) Almost 40, 000 people were arrested after March and files for 15, 000 of these survive, in which ordinary men speak in their own words. This is a unique source for making contact with those who normally leave no written trace in history. . . .

. . . The average man in the street wanted self-government for the capital: the abolition of the prefecture of police, the right to elect its municipal council and the officers of its national guard. He wanted popular sovereignty: the theory of direct government of the people, involving representatives elected for short periods and constantly revocable, was particularly favoured. Some looked on this as giving them an opportunity to hold public office, to obtain state jobs. To more, however, it was just a persistence of the ideal of 1793. Social antagonisms were distinctly vague. Though most of those arrested were wage-earners, and though they spoke vaguely against the rich, the bourgeoisie and the idle, they were not rebels against their employers, and there were practically no instances of class hostility against these. On the contrary, many got their employers to testify in their favour at their trials: the employer was an enemy only when he fled from Paris. On the whole, the people seemed to hate the clergy more than any other class; after that, their landlord, and then their *concierge*.

Theodore Zeldin, *France 1848–1945*, 1973, vol I, pp 738, 743

Questions

- *a* Why do Price and Zeldin regard the reports on the interrogations of the Communards as a particularly valuable source for arriving at a balanced view of the Commune? What is the nature of the 'simplification' (lines 70–1) which the reports help to correct?
- *b* Comment on the reliability of such interrogation reports as historical evidence. Should we accept the prisoners' statements at face value?
- *c* Explain what is meant by the 'ideal of 1793' (line 92).
- *d* What conclusions do Zeldin and Price draw from their study of the interrogation reports? Do their conclusions tally?
- *e* In what ways do the analyses presented by Zeldin and Price differ from that of Marx?
- * *f* Discuss the part played by women in the Commune.

5 The Significance of the Commune at its Centenary, 1971

Considerable attention has sometimes been given, and was given at the time in both Versailles and in more moderate Paris newspapers to the view that the Commune's basic objective was only to secure municipal autonomy within a republican form of government and that this was the
5 underlying issue in the civil war. . . . Undoubtedly the issue assumed a tactical importance in view of the success of the Thiers government in spreading in rural areas the spectre of a socialist Paris imposing expropriation and communism upon all Frenchmen. . . . This question actually emerged more because the revolution in Paris, after early April,
10 could succeed on no other basis. Once it became fairly evident that the existing national government was not going to be overthrown after all and that the Communal insurrections in other cities were defeated or facing defeat, the only possible objective – although few members of the Commune or Communards would have admitted this – was that of
15 securing a negotiated settlement that would at least guarantee a degree of municipal autonomy with which to effect some limited political and social reforms as well as guarantees of democratic liberties. However, were decentralisation the decisive issue in the civil war there would scarcely have been a raison d'être for the absolute resistance of both sides,
20 especially Versailles, to a negotiated peace nor for the extremely savage and prolonged repression that followed the defeat of the Commune. . . .

In spite of the heterogeneous mélange of democratic and socialist ideas, the concern with the immediate issue of defending the Commune and the absence of concrete programmes, there does appear to be one feature
25 fundamental in describing the entire Communal revolution: it is that the Commune's very existence, rather than the sum total of measures and statements, embodies its greatest historical significance. No matter how spontaneous its origins, how amorphous its direction and how im-

provised its actions, the Commune represents the first time in modern
30 history that a revolutionary government – freely elected by the majority of the voting population of a crucial section of a major European country – was composed in the main of workers or their associates and considered itself as serving primarily the working classes, and above all else, unequivocally substituted itself, under electoral control, for all
35 prevailing governmental, military, police, judicial and administrative structures – what today would be called the entire Establishment. To overlook this essential feature of the Commune is not to see the forest for the trees. If the Commune was indeed the last Jacobin revolution, it was simultaneously the first modern, or 'Left' revolution, in spite of the
40 absence of immediate socialist orientation.

Eugene Schulkind, *The Paris Commune of 1871*, Historical Association Pamphlet 78, 1971, pp 29–31, 33

Questions

* *a* Explain the following: (i) 'Communal insurrections in other cities' (line 12); (ii) 'heterogeneous mélange' (line 22).

* *b* Discuss Eugene Schulkind's assertion that the revolutionary government in Paris 'was composed in the main of workers or their associates and considered itself as serving primarily the working classes' (lines 32–3).

c Explain why Eugene Schulkind considers the Commune to be the first 'modern' revolution (line 39) in European history. Compare his view with Karl Marx's in extract 2.

d What arguments does Eugene Schulkind use to counter the apparent importance of the Commune's desire to secure Parisian municipal autonomy? How does the historian's assessment of the importance of this issue affect his interpretation of the significance of the Commune in the history of revolutions?

Further Work

a 'Far from being the model of a new era of proletarian revolution, the Commune was the last dying flicker of the old tradition. It looked not forward, but back.' (David Thomson) Discuss the causes and conduct of the Commune in the light of this statement.

b 'The Paris Commune represented the triumph of the countryside over the city, of the provinces over the capital.' Discuss.

c How far did class warfare affect domestic affairs in France between the suppression of the Commune and the outbreak of the First World War?

d Karl Marx believed that the Commune marked the beginning of an era of revolutions in Europe. Why was he wrong?

VII Railways and European Society in the Nineteenth Century

Introduction

The revolution in transport which was brought about by the spread of railways in the middle of the nineteenth century exerted an enormous influence on the economic and social life of Europe. The creation of the network of railways meant new demands on heavy industry to provide the raw materials of construction, new departures in the world of finance to provide the funds and new possibilities of employment for the expanding population as the labour force. Once built, the railways gave an essential stimulus to the industrial revolution in Europe, whilst the speed, ease and cheapness of travel by train opened new worlds to all whom the rails reached and helped to create new states out of a host of local communities. In the case of Germany, as David Thomson remarks, 'Just as the *Zollverein* removed the artificial impediments, so the railways removed the natural impediments to German integration and prosperity.'

No less significant were the effects of railways on the art of war. Now larger bodies of soldiers could be moved over greater distances at higher speeds, and the wear and tear of a long march no longer had to be taken into account. Armies could be supplied and reinforced once war had begun, but careful preparation was needed to ensure the smooth working of any operations dependent on railways. Little could safely be left to hasty improvisation, and in 1914 one military leader (see extract 6) was brought to a state of nervous collapse by the thought of what might happen if amateurs were allowed to meddle with the strategic plans on which his country's mobilisation schedules were based. It is one of the ironies of nineteenth-century history that the railways which had contributed so much to the increase in the prosperity of Europe should have played a significant part in bringing on the conflict which shattered it. A. J. P. Taylor writes of August 1914, 'The First World War had begun – imposed on the statesmen of Europe by railway timetables. It was an unexpected climax to the railway age.'

Further Reading

The economic and social effects of the railways can best be studied in the relevant volumes of *The New Cambridge Modern History*, *The Fontana Economic History of Europe* and *The Cambridge Economic History of Europe*.

For further documentary material, see Sidney Pollard and Colin Holmes (eds), *Documents of European Economic History* (Edward Arnold, 1972). For the effects of railways on war, see Sir Basil Liddell Hart's chapter on 'Armed Forces and the Art of War: Armies' in *The New Cambridge Modern History*, volume X, and Michael Howard's chapter on 'The Armed Forces' in volume XI. See also Michael Howard, *The Franco-Prussian War* (Hart-Davis, 1961) and *War in European History* (Oxford University Press, 1976).

1 Railways in Germany: Count Helmuth von Moltke, the future Field Marshal, writes to his brother in April 1844 from Berlin

This year we have a grand Review at Halle, so that I cannot get away till October. After last year's experiences, I dare not go to the Baltic or the North Sea for baths at that season, and that is why I thought of Nice, where I could bathe in the winter. Another plan was to go to England in
5 October, where one can still take sea baths, especially in the Isle of Wight. We should take that opportunity of seeing London and something of old England. I cannot say yet which of these plans, or indeed, if either of them can be carried out, and I find it very hard to choose between the palm groves of Aquitania and the art treasures of Britain. Marie would
10 probably prefer England, and of course we could only make this expensive journey so long as there are no children, who would either have to be left behind or make it still more expensive for us. One can always manage to get to the South, and I think we might some day go together to Switzerland, and to the orange gardens of the West.

15 Next year we shall be able to travel by rail from my door to Zürich, into the heart of the Swiss Alps. Even now, one can go in a single day from here to Zwickau by Leipzig and Altenburg, a distance of fifty miles [about 234 English miles], for a few thalers. In three years, there will, in all probability, be an unbroken line of railway from Kiel by Hamburg,
20 Berlin, Frankfurt, Breslau, Brünn, Vienna, Trieste, Venice, Milan. This is not a fantasy, for the line is partly finished, partly in process of construction. Ninety miles [about 491 English miles] of it can already be used. That is what we are doing in Germany. While the French Chambers are still engaged in discussing the matter, we have laid down three
25 hundred miles of railway and are working at two hundred more.

Amongst the latter is the Hamburg-Berlin line, to whose board of directors I belong. The greatest difficulty that we have still to contend with is the Danish Government. It wants to force us into keeping along the Elbe and through Lauenburg, which would cost us two million
30 thalers more than the route we had chosen by Schwarzenbeck. There is some talk of a deputation to Copenhagen, in which I am to take part, but

the matter may yet be settled by diplomacy. Meanwhile we have begun the line in Heaven's name and intend it to be finished in 1846.

Letters of Field Marshal Count Helmuth von Moltke to his Mother and his Brothers, 1891, volume II, pp 137–9

Questions

a What impression does this extract give of the reasons for von Moltke's enthusiasm for railway development in Europe at the time of writing this letter?

* *b* How did the growth of railways assist the process of creating a united Germany?

* *c* What part did railways play in von Moltke's military career?

* *d* What problems did the French encounter in developing their national railway network in the 1840s?

2 Railways and Nation-Building: Count Cavour on Italy's Railways, 1846

The railroad from Turin to Chambery . . . will be one of the wonders of the world; it will immortalise the name of King Charles Albert if he has the courage and and energy to build it. Incalculable benefits will follow, which will make eternal the memory of his reign, already marked by so
5 many glorious achievements. . . .

If the future holds a happy fortune for Italy, if this fair country, so one may hope, is destined to regain her nationality, it can only be the consequence of a remodelling of Europe, or as a result of one of those great providential explosions in which the mere ability to move troops by
10 rail will be unimportant. . . . A railway connection bringing Vienna and Milan within a few hours of each other cannot impede such a great event. That being so, a line from Vienna to Trieste is another whose construction is most to be desired; for it will immediately help Italian agriculture by opening many new outlets. . . .

15 So manifold are the attractions of our country that it is difficult to guess the number of foreigners who will one day seek here a purer and cleaner air for their impaired health. . . . That will be one undeniable gain from the railways. However we think it the least important benefit of all. . . . The presence of a great mass of foreigners in our midst is
20 undoubtedly a source of profit, but it has its own inconveniences. Relations between Italians on the one hand, and rich and leisured foreigners on the other, whom the local population will exploit in order to live – this will hardly favour the development of industrious, moral habits; it may engender a spirit of guile and servility which will damage
25 the national character. . . .

Once the network of railways is complete, Italy will begin to enjoy a considerable transit trade. . . . Railways will open a magnificent econ-

omic future for Italy. . . . Nevertheless, however great the material benefits to Italy from railways, they are much less important than the
30 inevitable moral effects. . . .

We are certain that the prime cause [of Italy's troubles] is the political influence which foreigners have exercised on us for centuries, and that the principal obstacles opposed to us throwing off this baleful influence are, first and foremost, the internal divisions, the rivalries, I might almost say,
35 the antipathy that different parts of our great Italian family hold for each other; and, following that, the reciprocal distrust which divides our rulers from the most energetic section of those they rule. . . . If the action of the railways diminishes these obstacles and perhaps even abolishes them, it will give the greatest encouragement to the spirit of Italian nationality.
40 Communications, which help the incessant movement of people in every direction, and which will force people into contact with those they do not know, should be a powerful help in destroying petty municipal passions born of ignorance and prejudice. . . .

This first moral consequence seems so great that it alone would justify
45 the enthusiasm felt for railways by all true friends of Italy; but there is a second moral effect, less easy to grasp, but still more important. . . . The history of the last thirty years, as well as an analysis of the various elements in Italian society, will prove that military or democratic revolutions can have little success in Italy. All true friends of the country must therefore
50 reject such means as useless. They must recognise that they cannot help their fatherland except by gathering in support of legitimate monarchs who have their roots in the national soil. . . . More than by any other administrative reform, as much perhaps as by liberal political concessions, the building of the railways will help to consolidate the mutual
55 confidence between governments and people, and this is the basis of our hopes for the future. These governments have the destiny of their peoples in trust, and railway building is therefore a powerful instrument of progress which testifies to the benevolent intentions of each government and the security they feel. On their side the people will be grateful for this
60 and will come to hold their sovereigns in complete trust; docile, but full of enthusiasm, they will let themselves be guided by their rulers in the acquisition of national independence.

Denis Mack Smith (ed.), *The Making of Italy 1796–1866*, 1968, pp 101–9

Questions

a What does Cavour mean by (i) 'the most energetic section of those they rule' (line 37); (ii) his reference to the lack of success of 'military or democratic revolutions' (line 48)?

b What 'material benefits' does Cavour see stemming from railway development in Italy? What possible 'moral' disadvantage does he envisage?

c How are Cavour's views on the true path to national unity revealed in this extract and how does he believe that railways will help foster this solution?

* *d* What reason does Cavour give for rejecting the military implications of railways? Was he correct to do so?

e What indications are there that Cavour was writing here to influence Charles Albert of Piedmont to support railway development in his kingdom? Was he successful?

3 Railways and War, 1859

It was in the Italian campaign of 1859 that railways first played a conspicuous part in actual warfare, both strategically and tactically. 'In this campaign,' said Major Millar of the Topographical Staff, in two lectures delivered by him at the Royal United Service Institution in 1861:

> 5 railways assisted the ordinary means of locomotion hitherto employed by armies. By them thousands of men were carried daily through France to Toulon, Marseilles, or the foot of Mont Cenis; by them troops were hastened up to the very fields of battle; and by them injured men were brought swiftly back to the hospitals, still groaning in the first agony of their wounds.
> 10 Moreover, the railway cuttings, embankments and bridges presented features of importance equal or superior to the ordinary accidents of the ground, and the possession of which was hotly contested. If you go to Magenta you will see, close to the railway platform on which you alight, an excavation full of rough mounds and simple black crosses, erected to mark the resting-places of many
> 15 hundred men who fell in the great fight. This first employment of railways in close connection with vast military operations would alone be enough to give a distinction to this campaign in military history.

The French railways, especially, attained a remarkable degree of success. . . . It was estimated that the 75,966 men and 4,469 horses
20 transported by rail from Paris to the Mediterranean or to the frontiers of the Kingdom of Sardinia between April 20 and April 30 would have taken sixty days to make the journey by road. In effect, the rate of transit by rail was six times greater than the rate of progress by marching would have been, and this, again, was about double as fast as the best
25 achievement recorded up to that time on the German railways. The Chasseurs de Vincennes are described as leaving the station at Turin full of vigour and activity, and with none of the fatigue or the reduction in numbers which would have occurred had they made the journey by road.

As against, however, the advantage thus gained by the quicker
30 transport of the French troops to the seat of war, due to the successful manner in which the railways were operated, there had to be set some serious defects in administrative organisation. When the men got to the end of their rail journey there was a more or less prolonged waiting for the food and other necessaries which were to follow. There were grave
35 deficiencies also, in the dispatch of the subsequent supplies. On June 25,

the day after the defeat of the Austrians, the French troops had no provisions at all for twenty-four hours, except some biscuits which were so mouldy that no one could eat them. Their horses, also, were without fodder. In these circumstances it was impossible to follow up the
40 Austrians in their retreat beyond the Mincio.

Thus the efficiency of the French railways was to a large extent negatived by the inefficiency of the military administration; and in these respects France had a foretaste, in 1859, of experiences to be repeated on a much graver scale in the Franco-German War of 1870–71.

45 As regards the Austrians, they improved but little on their admittedly poor performance in 1850, in spite of the lessons they appeared to have learned as the result of their experiences on that occasion. Government and railways were alike unprepared. Little or no attempt at organisation in time of peace had been made, and, in the result, trains were delayed or
50 blocked, and stations got choked with masses of supplies which could not be forwarded. . . .

Then, also, the good use made of the railways by the allies in carrying out their important flanking movement against the Austrians at Vercelli gave further evidence of the fact that rail-power was a new force which
55 could be employed, not alone for the earlier concentration of troops at the seat of war, but, also, in support of strategic developments on the battle-field itself.

Edwin A. Pratt, *The Rise of Rail-Power in War and Conquest 1833–1914*, 1915, pp 9–12

Questions

a How did the coming of railways affect the conduct of military operations in the mid-nineteenth century?

b In what ways did railways increase or decrease the hardships experienced by rank-and-file soldiers in wartime?

c How did the Italian war of 1859 demonstrate the growing importance of 'organisation in time of peace' (lines 48–9) for military campaigns?

* *d* What influence did the relative efficiency of the use of railways by Austrian, French and Prussian armies have on the outcome of the Seven Weeks' war in 1866 and the Franco-Prussian war in 1870?

4 Railways and the Farmer

It is quite clear that the development of manufacturing industry and cities would not have been possible without the creation of a transport system more advanced than that which existed under the Ancien Régime, and that such a system was found in the railways. These developments were
5 necessary for the progress of agriculture. . . . But it is not just a question of transporting bulky goods at a cheap rate. There is a good deal of farm produce which cannot be sent long distances. . . . It is well known that

great progress has been made in the transport of perishable goods during the last fifteen years by the application of the science of refrigeration.
10 Ships and refrigerator vans make it possible to transport meat and fruit for long distances; in the centres of consumption cold storage centres preserve these provisions for a further period. . . .

These observations might lead one to suppose that the modern organisation of transport has only brought benefit to farmers. . . . This is
15 not the case, as is well known. At the same time as the railways stimulated the growth of towns, i.e. the centres of consumption, as they extended the market for agricultural products and levelled out prices, they made possible the development of new agricultural areas, and the progress of the mercantile marine has brought before our peasants the spectre of
20 foreign competition. . . . While the locomotive provided the peasants with a national market, the development of communications brought about international competition and obliged them to sustain an unequal struggle.

M. Augé-Laribé, *L' Evolution de la France agricole*, 1912, in Sidney Pollard and Colin Holmes (eds), *Documents of European Economic History*, 1972, volume II, pp 41–2

Questions

a In what ways were economic and social changes stimulated by railway development advantageous to French peasant farmers in the nineteenth century?

* *b* Why did European farmers begin to experience foreign competition and what were its main sources? Why was it an 'unequal struggle'?

* *c* How did European farmers and their governments respond to the threat from foreign competition?

5 Railways and Changing Economic Conditions in the late Nineteenth Century

The year 1850 had been, as we have seen, that of the railway, and the vogue for railways persisted up to 1880. . . . The fact was that the business world was under the illusion that the mileage returns from lines built in 1880 would equal that of the lines built in 1850. Unfortunately, it
5 is quite obvious that branch lines of small secondary centres, on which moreover traffic was slower, could never bring in as much as the great main lines. In 1882 thousands of miles of track built by the French Government could not find a bidder, and the exchequer had to bear the cost until almost the end of the century. Furthermore, the *Compagnie de*
10 *l'Ouest*, for instance, managed its affairs so badly that it had to be nationalised in 1909. It was the same in Belgium; the state was obliged to buy back certain lines, and doubled its network in 1873; in 1880 it built three-quarters of the railways and almost completed the system in 1908.

In Germany the completion of the railway system had largely been
15 facilitated by the war indemnity paid by France. All the same the Prussian Government also had to buy back the networks of Hanover, Hesse and Nassau. The Imperial Government bought back the Alsace-Lorraine network and set up an organisation that by and large turned the railways into a state concern though it was opposed by some countries, among
20 them Bavaria. In Prussia the state lines increased from three thousand to nearly twenty-five thousand miles, while the private lines fell from something like eight thousand to less than two thousand. This concentration of railways in government hands is worth noting, since it could be considered the beginning of state capitalism. In the 1880s financiers were
25 continually complaining of the small profits now to be made on the railways. The fact was that the concentration of lines, the simplified and reduced rates, no longer made profits possible except for very large concerns. By 1900, only the very big French companies had come near to repaying the credits borrowed from the government. Only the Prussian
30 railways were bringing their owner, the government, substantial profits; moreover these remained outside parliamentary control and made possible a close connection between the railways and the military administrations. A similar situation was developing with the canals and roads; the age of individual enterprise on the English pattern of the 1830s
35 was definitely over. Only vast organised systems could meet the costs and guarantee profits. These hard facts were obvious only to a very small group of thinkers who met with such a hostile reception when they forecast the end of small-scale middle-class enterprise that they did not dare express openly their belief in 'state control' or their 'socialism'.

Charles Morazé, *The Triumph of the Middle Classes: A Study of European Values in the Nineteenth Century*, 1966, pp 377–8

Questions

a What parts were played by private enterprise and by government action in the initial development of railways in the various states of Europe?

* *b* Why did railways increasingly come under state ownership towards the end of the nineteenth century?

c What effects did railway development have on banking and finance in nineteenth-century Europe?

6 'War by Timetable', August 1914

(a) On 1 August 1914 the Kaiser, in the mistaken belief that the British Foreign Secretary, Sir Edward Grey, had indicated that Britain and France might remain neutral in event of war between Germany and Russia, told General von Moltke, Chief of the General Staff, 'Now we can go to war against Russia only. We simply march the whole of our Army to the East.' Von Moltke replied:

I assured His Majesty that this was not possible. The deployment of an army of a million men was not a matter of improvisation. It was the product of a whole year's work and, once worked out, could not be changed. If His Majesty insisted on leading the whole army eastwards, he would not have an army ready to strike, he would have a confused mass of disorderly armed men without commissariat. The Kaiser insisted on his demand and grew very angry, saying to me, amongst other things: 'Your uncle would have given me a different answer!' which hurt me very much. I have never claimed to be the equal of the Field-Marshal. Nobody seemed to reflect that it would bring disaster upon us if we were to invade Russia with our entire army, leaving a mobilised France in our rear. How, even with the best will, could England have prevented France from attacking us in the rear! In vain did I object that France was already mobilising and that a mobilised Germany and a mobilised France could not possibly come to an agreement to leave each other alone. The atmosphere grew more and more excited and I stood in a minority of one. I finally managed to persuade His Majesty that our concentration of strong forces against France and light defensive forces against Russia must be carried out as planned unless the most unholy muddle was to be created. I told the Kaiser that, once the concentration had been carried out, it would be possible to transfer forces at will to the eastern front, but that the concentration itself must proceed unchanged, or else I could not be responsible for things. . . .

In the course of this scene I nearly fell into despair. I regarded these diplomatic moves, which threatened to interfere with the carrying out of our mobilisation, as the greatest disaster for the impending war. . . . Years earlier the Foreign Ministry had told me that France might possibly remain neutral in a war between Germany and Russia. I had so little faith in this possibility that I said even then that, if Russia declared war on us, we should have to declare war on France at once were there the least doubt about her attitude.

(b) Von Moltke succeeded in convincing the Kaiser that the direction of the main German attack could not be altered, but the Kaiser then ordered that the army should remain within Germany's frontiers. Von Moltke continues:

As I stood there the Kaiser, without asking me, turned to the aide-de-camp on duty and commanded him to telegraph immediate instructions to the 16th Division at Trier not to march into Luxemburg. I thought my heart would break. The danger arose afresh that our concentration would be thrown into confusion. What that means can probably only be fully realised by one familiar with the complicated business of mobilisation, which has to be worked out down to the smallest details. Where every move is laid down in advance to the minute, any change cannot but have disastrous effects. I tried in vain to convince His Majesty that we needed and must secure the Luxemburg railways. I was snubbed with the remark that I should use other railways instead. The order must stand. Therewith

I was dismissed [from the Kaiser's presence]. It is impossible to describe the state of mind in which I returned home. I was absolutely broken and shed tears of despair.

Extracts from General von Moltke's Memoirs, given in Luigi Albertini, *The Origins of the War of 1914*, 1957, volume III, pp 172–6

Questions

a Explain the meaning of (i) the term 'commissariat' (line 6); (ii) the reference to 'the Field-Marshal' (line 9).

b In what ways did the kaiser attempt to halt the movement towards a general European war and why does von Moltke oppose any change or delay? Do you think von Moltke's attitude is based more on his political judgements than on military or logistical considerations connected with railway movements?

c What impression is given by these extracts of von Moltke's state of mind at the time and of his relationship with the kaiser? Compare this with von Jagow's comments in section IX, document 1.

VIII Conversations with the Chancellor: Bismarck's Germany, 1867–90

Introduction

When Bismarck came to look back on his own career in his memoirs, he produced, in A.J.P. Taylor's phrase, 'probably the most misleading work of autobiography ever written'. This section looks at the major issues of the period 1867 to 1890 not through Bismarck's own words, but in the form of statements attributed to him by his contemporaries as events unfolded. There is no shortage of such records, since as the German socialist, Philip Scheidemann, scornfully remarked, 'almost everybody who once drank a glass of wine at Bismarck's house, or smoked a cigar there, has written a book about it'. The historian has the task of assessing the value of such recorded remarks as evidence of Bismarck's character, motives and aims, bearing in mind the fallibility of human memory and the circumstances and relationship of the parties to the conversation.

Contemporaries stood in awe of Bismarck, that 'hysterical colossus' as Thomas Mann called him, and of his achievement in uniting Germany and then dominating the German and European political scene for two decades. But the course of German history in the fifty years after Bismarck's death cast an increasingly heavy shadow across his work. Writing in 1941, Professor Friedrich Foerster described it as an 'incontestable fact' that Bismarck was the 'source and the embodiment of the curse that has lain upon modern Germany'. Bismarck's reputation suffered in the same way as that of Napoleon III through the praise bestowed on him by the Nazis, who regarded themselves as his heirs. In July 1944 Ulrich von Hassell, the former German ambassador in Rome who had by then joined the opposition to Hitler, wrote of Bismarck, 'It is regrettable what a false picture of him we ourselves have given the world – that of the power-politician with cuirassier boots – in our childish joy over the fact that at last someone had made Germany a name to reckon with again. . . . In truth the highest diplomacy and great moderation were his real gifts.'

The idea of Bismarck as a moderate and as a restraining influence is one which sheds light on the place of both his domestic and foreign policies in the pattern of German history. As A.J.P. Taylor writes, Bismarck 'lived in an age of democracy and German power and he devoted his life to making these two forces as harmless as possible'. In proclaiming Germany a 'satiated power' after the war with France, Bismarck acted with great wisdom, but his role in curbing German democracy, in the sense of stifling the growth of responsible parliamentary government, must be looked on in a less favourable light. It has been pointed out that even Bismarck cannot be held solely accountable, and that neither amongst the mass of the people nor amongst the politicians themselves was there a strongly-held belief that all political power should derive from the parliamentary system. But nonetheless, in terms of Germany's political development, Bismarck's legacy, as Max Weber wrote in 1917, was to have 'left behind him a nation lacking in all and every political education, far below the level that they had reached in this respect twenty years earlier.'

Taking a long-term view of German history over the last hundred years, recent historians have emphasised the importance of Bismarck's 'U-turn', as it might now be called, in the years 1877 to 1879, when he ended the *Kulturkampf* and adopted protectionist and anti-socialist policies. This involved a breach with the National Liberals and the reduction of their influence in German political life. Fritz Stern comments on this aspect: 'Better than any other episode during his reign, Bismarck's struggle against the National Liberals demonstrated his willingness to apply the tactics of international conflict to domestic rivals. . . . The example set and the results achieved did great harm to the political future of Germany.' Professor Böhme has described the political, economic and social changes arising from Bismarck's actions during this period as 'a reorganisation which was equivalent to a new founding of the Reich' – but on a less sound basis than before.

In terms of German foreign relations it was also a turning point. First, in making the Dual Alliance with Austria in 1879 Bismarck began to involve Germany, in the intended interests of peace and security, in a series of formal alliances which helped to bring on disaster in 1914 when their management was left to his less skilful successors. Secondly, Bismarck's realignment with the conservative forces in the country led in the 1880s to his adoption of a colonial policy which marked the end of the period when Germany could truly present herself as a 'satiated power' and the beginnings of her 'world policy'. Combined with the example of the success of his three short wars in the 1860s and French bitterness at the loss of Alsace-Lorraine, Bismarck's legacy to Germany in foreign policy was no less fraught with danger than in domestic affairs. It was Germany's and Europe's misfortune that Bismarck was more successful in restraining the potentially beneficial trends in German life than the harmful ones.

Further Reading

A bibliography on Bismarck and Germany would in itself fill a book so this must necessarily be the most selective list of suggested reading in this volume. Standard biographies of Bismarck include Erich Eyck, *Bismarck and the German Empire* (Allen & Unwin 1950), A.J.P.Taylor, *Bismarck, the Man and the Statesman* (Hamish Hamilton, 1955) and W. N. Medlicott, *Bismarck and Modern Germany* (English Universities Press, 1965). Further documents on the period can be found in L.L. Snyder, *The Blood and Iron Chancellor* (Van Nostrand, 1967), J.C.G. Röhl (ed.), *From Bismarck to Hitler* (Longman, 1970) and W.N. Medlicott and Dorothy K. Coveney, *Bismarck and Europe* (Edward Arnold, 1971). Historical interpretations of the significance of Bismarck's work are looked at in Theodore S. Hamerow, *Otto von Bismarck: A Historical Assessment* (D.C. Heath & Co., 1962). A useful recent discussion of Bismarck's career, with notes on points where historians have reached different conclusions, is George O. Kent, *Bismarck and his Times* (Southern Illinois University Press, 1978). Another recent work which contains valuable general discussion of the period, as well as an examination of the particular aspect of high finance, is Fritz Stern, *Gold and Iron: Bismarck, Bleichröder and the Building of the German Empire* (Knopf, 1977).

1 War with France: a Mr Beatty-Kingston recollects words spoken to him by Bismarck on 22 September 1867

I do not believe for a moment that France will fight us alone, for reckoning that every Prussian is at least as good as every Frenchman, we are numerically stronger than she is. The attack must come from her; we shall never begin a war, if war there ever be, for we have nothing to gain.
5 Suppose France entirely conquered, and a Prussian garrison in Paris; what are we to do with our victory? We could not even decently take Alsace, for the Alsatians are become Frenchmen, and wish to remain so. Belgium we do not want; besides England guarantees her integrity. . . . If the French fight us alone they are lost; therefore, as they know this, they
10 seek for allies. Will they find them? I will tell you why I think not. France, the victor, would be a danger to everybody – Prussia to nobody. That is our strong point.

Heinrich von Poschinger, *Conversations with Prince Bismarck*, 1900, pp 85–7

Questions

* *a* 'We shall never begin a war' (lines 3–4). Explain how the Hohenzollern candidature led to war in 1870. Did France or Prussia bear the greater degree of responsibility for the outbreak of hostilities?
* *b* Why did Bismarck's assessment that France would have to face Prussia on her own in a war prove to be correct in 1870?
* *c* 'We could not even decently take Alsace' (lines 6–7). Had Bismarck changed his mind by 1871 and if so, why? If not, why was Alsace annexed?
* *d* 'We have nothing to gain' (line 4). In the light of recent work on the development of Bismarck's German policy after the defeat of Austria, could these remarks to Mr Beatty-Kingston in 1867 be sincere?

2 Dr Moritz Busch, Bismarck's publicist, records in his diary two conversations with the Chancellor on Economic and Social Problems

(a) [May 1879] He then said: 'But tell me what you think of the last debates in the Reichstag, and the position of the Customs Reform.'

I replied: 'Well, I think one may congratulate you on the commencement of victory in the matter. The manner in which you disposed of Delbrück, in the debate on the corn tariff was simply delightful. Why, that was a refutation, point by point.'

'Yes,' he replied, smiling, 'but we cannot say how things will go at the third reading. If it is not passed, I shall make a Cabinet question of it; and as the King will not let me go, we shall dissolve. They, however, would seem inclined to procrastinate; and, in that case, I am not yet certain whether we ought to dissolve. Another year can, perhaps, do no harm, and the elections may in the meantime turn out better. The Ultramontanes, with whom it is altogether impossible to come to any permanent understanding, will hardly support the revenue taxes. Then we must have a dissolution, as we regard the reform as a whole, from which no part can be dissevered.'

I asked if I might say that in the press. He said: 'I think not. Emphasise in detail the position of the Eighty-Eight (the Opposition) in their private and business capacities, to the iron tariff. How most of these gentlemen – lawyers, journalists, holders of funded property – are people who live upon fees, salaries, pensions, dividends; and, having no immediate connection with agriculture, are not personally affected, and have no experience, yet have most to say in the matter.'

'Who neither sow, nor reap, nor spin, as you said to Lasker,' I observed, 'and who are nevertheless fed and clad. Of course, you did not refer to them alone, but to the whole class.'

'Certainly,' he replied, 'write that, and hunt up the necessary personal information. That may prove useful as a means of clearing up the situation for the elections. It must be shown that the majority of our legislators are the people who have nothing to do with practical affairs, and have no eye, no ear, no sympathy for the interests which the Government, in this case, defends. . . .'

The article which the Chief had ordered appeared in No 22 of *Grenzboten*, under the title of 'Some Characteristics of the Minority in the Question of Tariff Reform'.

(b) On the 18th of January, 1881, I wrote to the Chief reminding him of my readiness to place myself at his disposal in case he wished to have any matter of importance discussed in the German or English press, and requesting information. . . .

I went to the Chancellor's palace at the appointed time, and I remained with him for an hour and a half. The Prince sat at his writing-table with

40 his face towards the door, and looked particularly well and hearty. He said: 'So you have come for material, but there is not much to give you. One thing occurs to me, however. I shall be very thankful to you if you would discuss my working-class insurance scheme in a friendly spirit. The Liberals do not show much disposition to take it up and their
45 newspapers attack my proposals. The Government should not interfere in such matters – laisser aller. The question must be raised, however, and the present proposal is only the beginning. I have more in view. I grant that there may be room for improvement in many respects, and that some portions of the scheme are perhaps unpractical and should therefore be
50 dropped. But a beginning must be made with the task of reconciling the labouring classes with the State. Whoever has a pension assured to him for his old age is much more contented and easier to manage than the man who has no such prospect. Compare a servant in a private house and one attached to a Government office or to the Court; the latter, because he
55 looks forward to a pension, will put up with a great deal more and show much more zeal than the former. In France all sensible members of the poorer classes, when they are in a position to lay by anything, make a provision for the future by investing in securities. Something of the kind should be arranged by our workers. People call this State Socialism, and
60 having done so think they have disposed of the question. It may be State Socialism, but it is necessary. . . .'

I then took leave of him, and immediately wrote the first of the two articles he described, which appeared in the *Grenzboten*, No 5, of 1881, under the title 'Working-class Insurance Bill'.

Dr Moritz Busch, *Bismarck: Some Secret Pages of his History*, 1898, vol II, pp 397–400, 450–6

Questions

a Identify (i) Delbrück (line 6); (ii) Lasker (line 25).

b Explain the following: (i) 'I shall make a cabinet question of it' (line 9); (ii) 'The Ultramontanes' (line 14); (iii) 'Eighty-Eight' (line 19); (iv) 'laisser aller' (line 46).

* *c* What was the nature of the 'Customs Reform' (lines 2–3)? Discuss the possible reasons why Bismarck reversed his policy on tariffs in the late 1870s.

* *d* What reasons does Bismarck give for adopting a working-class insurance scheme? How successful were Bismarck's domestic policies as a whole in 'reconciling the labouring classes with the state' in the 1880s?

e What picture emerges from these extracts of Dr Busch and his relationship with Bismarck? How does this affect your treatment of them as historical source material?

f What do these extracts tell us about Bismarck's attitude to his political opponents and to the press?

3 Prince von Bülow recalls a breakfast-time talk with Bismarck in July 1884 at Bismarck's estate at Varzin

As I sat next morning in my room, eating a very large and excellent breakfast, the Prince entered. He sat down opposite me with the words: 'Don't let me disturb you, go on eating your eggs. I hope they have been boiled properly.' Then he continued, 'You are probably furious at being
5 sent to St Petersburg instead of to London? London is certainly pleasanter to live in. And I don't suppose it's easy for you to leave Paris. However you feel, you are putting a very good face upon it and not acting the injured party, and that's always the cleverest thing to do. . . .'

The Prince . . . then began to talk foreign policy. 'Our policy is
10 and remains a policy of peace. We have no reason to want a war, and I do not see what we should have to gain by one. The annexation of German-Austria, or the Baltic provinces, or even any Dutch or Swiss territory, would only weaken us. And so-called 'prophylactic' wars, that is, the policy of attacking someone else so that he may not grow a little
15 stronger and attack first, I consider, as did your father, who would have told you this, not only un-Christian but politically foolish as well. What did Napoleon I ever accomplish with his 'prophylactic' wars? One can always begin a war but one never knows how it may end! Three times God has given us victory. That was a great mercy. But to let it come to a
20 fourth war, without pressing reasons, would be tantamount to tempting Providence. It is in our own interests. Of course we must keep our sword sharp. Our political position, power, honour and wealth we owe in the first place to the army. The army also ensures monarchical government as the only solid basis of the realm, of order and our growing prosperity.
25 The pivot of our position, and with that of our whole policy, the point on which things turn, is our relationship to Russia. The French will only attack us if we let ourselves get embroiled with Russia, but then are certain to do so. As for the English, they have no reason at all for attacking us, even if they are beginning to envy our industrial and commercial
30 progress. . . .

For us, therefore, St Petersburg is now the most important diplomatic post. That is why I have transferred you there. . . . Point out wherever you can in St Petersburg that nobody can know how a military clash between the three imperial powers might end. One thing is certain. The
35 three dynasties, the three monarchs, would probably pay the penalty and the only real victor would be the revolution. Napoleon said on St Helena that Europe, after his fall, would be either Cossack or Republican. I believe that if the Prussian and the Cossack ever come to blows Europe will become Republican. The ticklish factor in our connections with
40 Russia is of course Austria. We cannot let Austria be overrun and shattered. But just as little must we let ourselves be dragged into war by her. To manoeuvre between these two crags is a matter of skill and a clear head, much the same qualities as are necessary to prevent two trains meeting in a head-on crash. . . .'

45 I had listened with the closest attention, and with boundless admiration. But I did not let my breakfast be interrupted and ate my eggs, the toast, and a smoked herring, which the kind Princess had ordered to be brought me, in comfort. That afternoon I went for a walk with Bill, he said to me, 'You will be glad to hear that my father said some nice things
50 about you. It pleased him especially that you went on calmly eating your eggs, "He has good nerves," he said, "he pleases me altogether."'

Memoirs of Prince von Bülow, 1932, vol IV, pp 555–8

Questions

* *a* Who was Prince von Bülow? Briefly outline his subsequent career.

b What does Bismarck mean by 'prophylactic' wars (line 13) and why does he reject them? Are there any cases where religious scruples (line 16) can actually be seen to have influenced Bismarck's policies?

c What reasons does Bismarck give for saying that St Petersburg is the 'most important diplomatic post' (lines 31–2)?

* *d* How successful was Bismarck in manoeuvring between the 'two crags' of Russia and Austria and preventing a 'head-on crash' in the period 1871–90?

e What impression does the reader get from this extract of Bismarck, von Bülow and the relationship between them? What reservations might there be about accepting von Bülow's account?

4 Prince von Bülow recalls Bismarck's comments on his 'domestic enemies' at Varzin, July 1884

In my presence and in the bosom of his family, he expressed some violent opinions of his domestic enemies. He did not want in the least to govern autocratically, he said, although the reproach was daily levelled against him. Real autocracy would be very different from the present govern-
5 ment in Germany. He was perfectly well aware that, in Germany, in the second half of the nineteenth century, absolutism and autocracy would be impossible, apart from the fact that such government had never been one of his ideals. But a parliamentary regime seemed to him just as impossible. Our parties possessed neither the patriotism of the French nor the
10 commonsense of the English. Under the circumstances he did not understand what benefits the German Liberals promised themselves from the 'inauguration of responsible ministries of the realm', which they had lately adopted as part of their programme. As long as he remained in office he would never countenance such a thing. Considering the political
15 incapacity of the average German, the intellectual parliamentary system would lead to conditions such as had prevailed in 1848, that is to say, to weakness and incompetency on the top, and to bumptiousness and ever new demands from below.

Memories of Prince von Bülow, 1932, vol IV, p 558

Questions

* *a* Bismarck here expresses the view that both autocracy and a parliamentary system are impossible in Germany: what kind of government had the constitution of 1871 given the new empire?

* *b* What were the main political parties in Germany in the period 1871 to 1890 of which Bismarck speaks so scathingly? Which in Bismarck's eyes would have seemed particularly lacking in 'patriotism' and 'commonsense' (lines 9–10)?

* *c* How would the political system desired by the Liberals have differed from the existing one? Why does Bismarck oppose this? Does the responsibility for the fact that no such system came into being rest solely with Bismarck?

d What picture does this extract give of Bismarck's attitude to his political opponents and his fellow countrymen?

5 Bismarck expounds his Colonial Policies

(a) *Berlin 22 February 1880* In the evening dined with Bismarck. I mentioned the fear that must be entertained of Gambetta. He attached no great importance to this, and said it could not be altered if it was so. At table much port and Hungarian wine was drunk. Afterwards I sat down 5 by the Chancellor and entered on a variety of subjects. He will not hear of colonies, now as at other times. He says we have not an adequate fleet to protect them, and our bureaucracy is not skilful enough to direct the management of them. He also spoke of my reports on the French designs on Morocco, and declared we could only be pleased if France took 10 possession of the country. Then it would have a great deal to do, and we could concede it the extension of its sphere in Africa as a set-off to Alsace-Lorraine. But when I asked whether I should declare myself to Freycinet to that effect he said no; that would be going too far.

Memoirs of Prince Chlodwig of Hohenlohe, 1906, vol II, p 259

15 (b) *6 June 1884* The colonial question, now in its early stages, may bedevil our relations with England for a considerable period, even though an actual conflict is out of the question. The problem is likely to pass over unsolved into the new reign. But should a conflict arise, no other question is so liable to put the future Kaiserin, with her Anglophile tendencies, in a 20 false position vis-à-vis the German nation. For it is precisely the liberals and democrats who want colonies.

I am far from supposing that this is the reason why the Chancellor has suddenly made the colonial question, to which he was so long opposed, a part of his political programme. But I am firmly convinced that, if the 25 need arises, he will use it as a means of combating foreign influences, and I am also convinced that he will succeed.

19 September 1884 Prince Bismarck told Tsar Alexander in Skierniewice

that the sole aim of German colonial policy was to drive a wedge between the Crown Prince and England. The Tsar, who had just been saying how
30 anxious he was about the fate of Russo-German relations after the death of Kaiser Wilhelm, remarked, '*Voilà qui est intelligent.*' I think for my part that all this colonial policy was undertaken simply as an election stunt. First came our victories, then the *Kulturkampf* and liberalism, then the economic revolution, and now colonies. Prince Bismarck said recently to
35 Bötticher (who cannot hold his tongue): 'All this colonial business is a fraud, but we need it for the elections!'

Some years ago Prince Bismarck said to me, and to many others: 'So long as I remain Minister we pursue no colonial policy.' Whether he has decided to do so for one or other of the reasons mentioned above, it is
40 nevertheless a fact that he does not pursue this colonial policy with his former vigour. Otherwise he would have adopted, i.e. would still adopt, far more decisive measures against England. His most recent habit is to clench his fist more often than he used to, but without dealing a blow.

The Papers of Friedrich von Holstein, 1957, vol II, pp 155, 161–2

Questions

* *a* Identify Gambetta (line 2) and Freycinet (line 12). Why was Hohenlohe alarmed by Gambetta?

b What is Bismarck's view on the German acquisition of colonies in 1880 and why?

* *c* Explain Holstein's reference to three earlier election 'stunts' (lines 32–4): (i) 'our victories'; (ii) 'the *Kulturkampf* and liberalism'; (iii) 'the economic revolution'.

d Explain the motives Bismarck had been heard to express for adopting a colonial policy in 1884.

e Why does Holstein believe that Bismarck's colonial policy is not a matter of deep conviction?

* *f* Are Bismarck's reported remarks an adequate explanation of his decision to adopt a colonial policy? Are there any other factors which may have influenced his change of course?

g What contribution do these extracts make to your picture of Bismarck's personality and political outlook?

6 Bismarck discusses his Dismissal with a Bavarian Newspaper Editor, 16 August 1890

My dismissal was not a thing of yesterday. I had long seen it coming. The Emperor wished to be his own Chancellor, with no one intervening between his Ministers and himself. He possesses the best intentions, talent, ambition and energy. But he is influenced by irresponsible people, makes
5 up his mind too quickly, and then forges ahead. His flatterers applaud, though behind his back they criticise without mercy. I am not angry with

him, far from it, but with these gentlemen you can use a thick stick. Sooner or later he will learn from experience, and you must not make it more difficult by insults to do so. Tell him the truth: he will take it better
10 from the press than he ever could from me. There were disagreements at the beginning of his reign, though on the major issues of European policy we were at one. But then there came a change and other influences were at work. He had ideas, both in domestic and foreign policy, which I could not approve. And our characters did not harmonise. The old Emperor
15 asked my opinion about everything of importance and told me his own. The young one consulted other people and wished to decide for himself. He wanted to be rid of me. I, too, wanted to go, though not just at the moment when he despatched two messengers to hurry me up. Matters of importance for the Reich were in progress, and I did not wish to see my
20 achievements of a quarter of a century scattered like chaff before the wind. Yet I am not angry with him, nor perhaps he with me. Broadly speaking my successor is carrying on my policy; for the moment he has no choice. Yet I fear it may not last, for he cannot stand up to the doctrinaire influences of the Emperor's entourage.

G. P. Gooch, *Studies in German History*, 1948, p 382

Questions

* *a* What were the principal issues in 'domestic and foreign policy' (line 13) about which Bismarck and the kaiser disagreed?

b What reasons does Bismarck give to explain his dismissal? Do you think that policies or personalities were more important?

* *c* Suggest what Bismarck has in mind when he refers to 'other influences' (line 12) and 'doctrinaire influences' (line 24).

* *d* What were the 'matters of importance for the Reich' to which Bismarck refers (lines 18–9)?

e Compare Bismarck's attitude to the press shown here with that in the conversations with Dr Busch.

* *f* Do you think Bismarck's apparent magnanimity in this extract is in keeping with his character as revealed in the other utterances in this section? What other evidence is there on his reaction to his dismissal?

Further Work

a What picture emerges of Bismarck, 'the man and the statesman', from these conversations and remarks?

b Imagine you are Bismarck speaking to a group of close friends just after your dismissal in 1890: how would you describe to them the main achievements of your years in office since 1867? What mistakes would you acknowledge?

c What advantages and pitfalls are there for historians in using the reported words of 'great men' as an historical source? Give examples from the above extracts to support your arguments.

IX The Outbreak of the First World War: Soldiers and Statesmen, 1914

Introduction

The controversy over who or what caused the First World War broke out almost as soon as the war had begun in 1914. To ensure the support of their own populations and of neutral countries, all governments vigorously maintained that the war had been forced upon them and that they were acting purely defensively. To the victors in 1918 went the privilege of allocating blame and in clause 231 of the Treaty of Versailles they spoke of the war as having been 'imposed upon them by the aggression of Germany and her Allies'. Between the wars, however, this verdict was gradually modified until a general agreement was reached that there were no guilty parties and that, in Lloyd George's words, Europe had sadly 'stumbled into the war'.

This consensus survived the Second World War, even though Germany's responsibility for that was taken for granted. In 1951 a group of German and French historians still supported the conclusion that 'the documents do not permit attributing a premeditated desire for a European war on the part of any government or people in 1914'. Economic, social and psychological factors were identified as the deeper currents dragging Europe towards the abyss, so that it seemed unreasonable to point an accusing finger at any group or individual acting against such a background in 1914. Then in the 1960s an historian from Hamburg, Fritz Fischer, did just that. Concentrating principally on an examination of German war aims in the First World War, he initially put forward the view that German actions in 1914 were based on an acceptance of the risk of war. In 1969 Fischer went further and claimed that Germany had prepared for a war of conquest and provoked it in 1914 before Russia became too strong. A heated debate ensued and still continues, with German historians such as Gerhard Ritter accusing Fischer of bias and distortion in resurrecting the idea of German 'war-guilt' in the context of 1914.

This section concentrates on the decisions taken in the last few weeks of peace in 1914, and looks particularly at the relationship between the civilian and military leaders and the pressures which they faced and to which they subjected each other. The documents bring out the importance of military plans and mobilisation systems in accelerating the slide from diplomacy to war and ensuring that any conflict would be a general war and not a local one. What few, if any, of the decision-makers in 1914 comprehended was that it would not only be a general European war but a world-wide struggle lasting four years and costing millions of lives. Any attempt to establish why the First World War could have been allowed to break out must contain an appreciation of the fact that the fateful decisions of July 1914 were taken in ignorance of the appalling nature of total war in the twentieth century.

Further Reading

Historians' views on the causes of the First World War can best be studied in two volumes: Dwight E. Lee (ed.), *The Outbreak of the First World War: Who was Responsible*? (Harrap, 1958) and H. W. Koch (ed.), *The Origins of the First World War* (Macmillan, 1972). Further documents can be found in Imanuel Geiss (ed.), *The Outbreak of the First World War: Selected Documents*; (1965; Batsford, 1967) and J. C. G. Röhl (ed.), *From Bismarck to Hitler* (Longman, 1970). The three books by Fritz Fischer which rekindled the controversy over Germany's role are *Germany's Aims in the First World War* (1961; Chatto & Windus, 1967), *World Power or Decline: the Controversy over Germany's aims in the First World War* (1965; Weidenfeld & Nicolson, 1974) and *War of Illusions: German policies from 1911 to 1914* (1969; Chatto & Windus, 1975). The role of militarism and military plans in hastening the outbreak of war is covered by Gerhard Ritter, *The Schlieffen Plan* (Wolft, 1958) and *The Sword and the Sceptre: the Problem of Militarism in Germany* (Penguin, 1972). On the same aspect see also Gordon A. Craig, *The Politics of the Prussian Army 1640–1945* (Oxford University Press, 1964) and Edward M. Earle (ed.), *The Makers of Modern Strategy* (Princeton University Press, 1961).

1 Germany: Early Summer 1914

Gottlieb von Jagow, the German Foreign Secretary, recalls a conversation with General von Moltke, Chief of the General Staff, in late May or early June 1914

Moltke described to me his opinion of our military situation. The prospects of the future oppressed him heavily. . . . In his opinion there
5 was no alternative to making preventive war in order to defeat the enemy while we still had a chance of victory. The Chief of General Staff therefore proposed that I should conduct a policy with the aim of provoking a war in the near future.

Moltke was not a man who lusted after the laurels of war. . . . Moltke
10 was a man who took his responsibilities very seriously but who rather suffered from the feeling that he was not quite up to the job – he was lacking in strategical genius. If he now pleaded for war, this must be because of his overwhelming concern about the growing superiority of our foes.

15 I countered that I was not prepared to cause a preventive war. . . . I

was not, on the other hand, blind to the gravity of our position. . . . A preventive war would become the unavoidable duty of farsighted politicians in certain circumstances as a defensive war. . . . If war seems unavoidable, one should not allow the enemy to dictate the moment, but to decide that
20 oneself. . . . But, quite apart from the fact that the suitable moment had perhaps passed already (at the formation of the Triple Entente, and in 1908–9, when Russia was notoriously still unprepared for war), I still had the hope that our relationship with England would improve to the extent that a general war would be virtually excluded, or at least rendered
25 less dangerous. For once they could no longer reckon with England's active support, the Russians and the French would hardly be tempted, without this backing, to provoke a military conflict with us. Germany would automatically become even stronger and more difficult to defeat if the peaceful development of her economic position continued. Apart
30 from defending ourselves from our enemies we had no 'war aims', such as conquests, etc, which would justify the heavy loss of life. Finally, I was not free from concern for internal reasons with regard to war: because of the character of the Supreme War Lord. And the Kaiser, who wanted to preserve peace, would always try to avoid war and only agree to fight if
35 our enemies forced war upon us.

After my rejection, Moltke did not insist further with his suggestion. The idea of a war was, as already mentioned, not liked by him.

When war did break out, unexpectedly and *not* desired by us, Moltke was . . . very nervous and obviously suffering from strong depression. In
40 July 1914, too, I hoped that a general war would be avoided. But I cannot deny that the memory of Moltke's opinion as expressed in this conversation gave me some confidence in a victory, should such a war prove unavoidable.

E. Zechlin, 'Motive und Taktik der Reichsleitung 1914', *Der Monat*, 209, February 1966, in J. C. G. Röhl (ed.), *From Bismarck to Hitler*, 1970, pp 70–1

Questions

a What account is given here of von Moltke's assessment of Germany's military situation in the summer of 1914? What course of action does this lead him to advocate?

b Explain the distinction between a 'defensive' and a 'preventive' war (lines 17–18).

c What arguments does von Jagow say that he put forward to counter von Moltke's call for a preventive war? Do you think his account of his position in 1914, written after the First World War, is open to question?

d Comment on von Jagow's statements that Germany had 'no "war aims", such as conquests' (lines 30–1) and that the Kaiser 'wanted to preserve peace' (lines 33–4).

e 'I hoped that a general war would be avoided.' (line 40). What significance would you attach to von Jagow's use of the word 'general' here?

* *f* 'If war seems unavoidable. . . .' (lines 18–19). What does this extract tell us about the state of relations between the great powers of Europe in 1914? How had this situation come about?

2 Austria: 12 July 1914

Conrad von Hötzendorf, Chief of the Austrian General Staff, writes to Count von Berchtold, Austrian Foreign Minister, on 12 July 1914 regarding the ultimatum to Serbia

In my capacity as Chief of the General Staff I am only concerned with the exact terms of the decision, whether directly aiming at the outbreak of a war with Serbia or only reckoning with the possibility of a war. The diplomatic handling of either alternative lies, of course, outside my province; I must however again point out, as I explained verbally to Your Excellency with your complete approval, that in the diplomatic field everything must be avoided in the nature of protracted or piecemeal diplomatic action which would afford our adversary time for military measures and place us at a military disadvantage. . . . Hence it would be wise to avoid everything that might prematurely alarm our adversary and lead him to take counter-measures; in all respects a peaceable appearance should be displayed. But once the decision to act has been taken, military considerations demand that it must be carried out in a single move with a short-term ultimatum which, if rejected, should be followed immediately by the mobilisation order.

Conrad von Hötzendorf, *Aus Miener Dienstzeit 1906–18*, 1921–5, vol IV, p 78, in Luigi Albertini, *The Origins of the War of 1914*, 1953, vol II, p 173

Questions

a What is 'the decision' (line 2) with which von Hötzendorf is concerned here?

b Although von Hötzendorf claims that diplomatic actions are outside his province, how does he seek to influence them?

c What effects are von Hötzendorf's 'military considerations' (lines 13–14) likely to have on the scope for diplomacy in the crisis that was developing?

* *d* Explain the circumstances which led to the Austrian ultimatum to Serbia. Was von Hötzendorf's advice followed in the Austrian handling of the ultimatum?

* *e* 'It is doubtful whether a major European power ever before stumbled into a war for survival struck with such blindness.' Do you think this is a fair assessment of decisions taken by the leaders of Austria in 1914?

3 France: 29 July 1914

Raymond Poincaré, President of France, returning from his visit to Russia, landed at Dunkirk on 29 July 1914

It was really France waiting for us and coming to meet us. I felt I was pale with emotion and made an effort not to show my emotion. . . . What struck me was that many people here seem to think war imminent. . . . One of those speaking to me, a man of some importance . . . went so far as to say me: 'We have had enough of this! . . . Better make an end of it once and for all.' I calmed him, answering: 'For mercy's sake, do not talk like that. We must still do everything to avoid war.'

[On reaching Paris] before we emerged on to the square [Messimy, the Minister for War] said to me, 'Monsieur le Président, you are going to see Paris; it is magnificent.' Indeed it was magnificent. . . . I was greeted by an overwhelming demonstration which moved me to the depths of my being. Many people had tears in their eyes and I could hardly hold back my own. From thousands of throats arose repeated shouts of: '*Vive la France! Vive la République! Vive le Président!*'. . . From the station to the Elysée the cheering never stopped. . . . Never have I felt so overwhelmed. Never have I found it more difficult, morally and physically, to maintain an impassive bearing. Greatness, simplicity, enthusiasm, seriousness, all combined to render this welcome unexpected, unbelievable and infinitely beautiful. Here was a united France. Political quarrels were forgotten.

Raymond Poincaré, *Au Service de la France. Neuf Années de Souvenirs*, 1926–33, vol IV, pp 361–9, in Luigi Albertini, *The Origins of the War of 1914*, 1953, vol II, pp 595–6

Questions

* *a* Why had Poincaré visited Russia? Did the visit have any results?

b Comment on the mood of the French people shown in this extract. What was Poincaré's reaction to this reception?

* *c* Suggest reasons for the 'enthusiasm' (line 20) of the French people in this crisis. Were similar sentiments to be seen in other European countries?

d Comment on the last sentence of this extract.

* *e* What responsibility did France have for the outbreak of the war?

4 Russia: 30 July 1914

(a) Serge Sazonov, the Russian Foreign Minister, recalls in his memoirs his audience with the Tsar on 30 July 1914

The Tsar was alone, and I was at once admitted to his study. I noticed at the first glance that he was tired and anxious. After greeting me he asked whether I had anything against General Tatishtchev being present at our interview. . . . I answered that I should be very pleased. . . . I began my report at ten minutes past three and finished at four. I told the Tsar in detail my conversation with the Minister of War and the Chief of the General Staff, omitting nothing of what I had heard from them and mentioning the last news that had been received at the Ministry of Foreign affairs from Austria and Germany and were still unknown to His Majesty. This news left no doubt whatever that during the two days I had not seen the Emperor the position had changed so much for the worse that there was no more hope of preserving peace. All our conciliatory offers, which went far beyond anything that a Great Power, whose resources were still untouched, could be expected to concede, had been rejected. . . . I told the Tsar that I fully agreed with Yanushkevich and Sukhomlinov that it was dangerous to delay the general mobilisation any longer, since, according to the information they possessed, the German mobilisation, though not as yet proclaimed officially, was fairly advanced. . . .

On the morning of July 30 the Tsar had received a telegram from the Emperor Wilhelm saying that if Russia continued to mobilise against Austria the Kaiser would be unable to intercede, as the Tsar had asked him. The decision rested, therefore, with the Tsar, who had alone to bear the responsibility for war or for peace. . . . I could see from his expression how wounded he was by its tone and content. . . . After giving me time to read the unfortunate telegram carefully, the Tsar said, in an agitated voice: 'He is asking the impossible. He has forgotten, or does not wish to remember, that the Austrian mobilisation had begun sooner than the Russian, and now asks us to stop ours without saying a word about the Austrian. You know I have already suppressed one mobilisation decree and then consented only to a partial one. If I agreed to Germany's demands now, we should find ourselves unarmed against the Austrian Army which is mobilised already. It would be madness.'. . .

In the circumstances there was nothing left for the Tsar but to give orders for general mobilisation. The Tsar was silent. Then he said to me, in a voice full of deep feeling: 'This would mean sending hundreds of thousands of Russian people to their death. How can one help hesitating to take such a step?' I answered that the responsibility for the precious lives carried away by the war would not fall upon him. Neither he nor his government desired the war . . . thrust upon Russia and Europe by the ill-will of the enemy, determined to increase their power by enslaving our natural Allies in the Balkans, destroying our influence there and reducing Russia to a pitiful dependence upon the arbitrary will of the Central Powers. . . .

I had nothing further to add and sat opposite the Tsar, watching him intently. He was pale and his expression betrayed a terrible inner struggle. I was almost as agitated as he. . . . General Tatishtchev was sitting next to me; he had not uttered a word, but was, like me, in a condition of unbearable moral tension. At last the Tsar said, speaking as it were with difficulty: 'You are right. There is nothing left us but to get ready for an attack upon us. Give then the Chief of the General Staff my order for mobilisation.'

55 Serge Sazonov, *Fateful Years 1909–16*, 1928, pp 201–5

(b) An account of the same meeting by Baron Schilling, chief secretary at the Russian Foreign Office; Schilling based it on his diary notes of Sazonov's comments on returning from the audience

During the course of nearly an hour the Minister proceeded to show that
60 war was becoming inevitable, as it was clear to everybody that Germany had decided to bring about a collision, as otherwise she would not have rejected all the pacificatory proposals that had been made and could easily have brought her ally to reason. Under these circumstances it only remained to do everything that was necessary to meet war fully armed
65 and under the most favourable conditions for ourselves. Therefore it was better to put away any fears that our warlike preparations would bring about a war, and to continue these preparations carefully rather than by reason of such fears to be taken unawares by war.

The firm desire of the Tsar to avoid war at all costs, the horrors of
70 which filled him with repulsion, led His Majesty in his full realisation of the heavy responsibility which he took upon himself in this fateful hour to explore every possible means for averting the approaching danger. Consequently he refused during a long time to agree to the adoption of measures which, however indispensable from a military point of view,
75 were calculated, as he clearly saw, to hasten a decision in an undesirable sense.

The tenseness of feeling experienced by the Tsar at this time found expression, amongst other signs, in the irritability most unusual with him, with which His Majesty interrupted General Tatistchev. The latter,
80 who throughout had taken no part in the conversation, said in a moment of silence: 'Yes, it is hard to decide.' His Majesty replied in a rough and displeased tone: 'I will decide' – in order by this means to prevent the General from intervening any further in the conversation.

Finally the Tsar agreed that under existing circumstances it would be
85 very dangerous not to make timely preparations for what was apparently an inevitable war, and therefore gave his decision in favour of an immediate general mobilisation.

Baron Schilling, *How the War began in 1914*, 1925, pp 64–6

Questions

* *a* '[T]here was no more hope of preserving peace' (line 14). What considerations would have influenced Sazonov in reaching this conclusion on 30 July 1914?

* *b* 'All our conciliatory offers' (lines 13–15). Did Russia make such gestures in 1914?

c What is Sazonov's purpose in seeking this audience with the tsar?

What arguments does he use to obtain the decision he wants from Nicholas?

d Why did the tsar find the decision on mobilisation such a difficult one to take? What do these extracts tell us about the tsar's state of mind when he took the decision?

e Are there any differences between these two accounts of the same episode? Comment on the reliability of the two versions.

* *f* In what ways did Russian policy in 1914 contribute to the outbreak of the First World War?

5 Germany: 30 July 1914

The German Chancellor, Bethmann Hollweg, reflects on Germany's position following Russia's announcement of general mobilisation on 30 July 1914:

We were not in complete agreement among ourselves as to how we were to proceed officially. The War Minister, General von Falkenhayn, thought it was a mistake to declare war on Russia, not because he considered that war could be avoided after Russia had mobilised, but because he feared that the political effect would be prejudicial to us. The Chief of the General Staff, General von Moltke, was on the other hand in favour of declaring war, because our plan of mobilisation, providing for a war on two fronts, required that military actions be immediately taken, and because our hope of success against an enormous superiority in numbers was dependent on the extreme rapidity of our movements. I myself agreed with the view of General von Moltke. I was, of course, under no illusion as to the effect on the question of responsibility for the war that our declaration would have and actually did have. But it was impossible at a moment when the existence of the country was entirely dependent on military action to oppose the military arguments, quite reasonable in themselves, of that general who was responsible for military operations. The unanimity of the German people was in no way impaired by the declaration of war against Russia. . . .

Our invasion of Belgium has been generally considered as of crucial importance in the course of the universal catastrophe. . . . Our military men, as far as I know, had had for long only one plan of campaign which was based on the unmistakable and unmistaken assumption that a war for Germany must be a war on two fronts. The plan of campaign was – the most rapid offensive in the West, and, during its first period, a defensive in the East. A strategy on these lines seemed to offer the only possibility of making head against the enemy's superior strength. But military opinion held that a condition of success for the Western offensive was passage through Belgium. Herein, political and military interests came into sharp conflict. The offence against Belgium was obvious, and the general political consequences of such an offence were in no way obscure. The chief of the General Staff, General von Moltke, was not blind to this consideration, but declared that it was a case of absolute military necessity. I had to accommodate my view to his. No observer who was in any way in his sober senses could overlook the immense peril of a war on 35 two fronts, and it would have been too heavy a burden of responsibility for a civilian authority to have thwarted a military plan that had been elaborated in every detail and declared to be essential. For this would later have been looked on as the sole cause of any catastrophe that might supervene.

Bethmann Hollweg, *Reflections on the World War*, 1920, pp 137–47

Questions

a How do the German leaders differ as to the correct course of action on 30 July 1914?

b What factors led Bethmann Hollweg to side with von Moltke?

c What were the possible dangers for Germany in taking the initiative of declaring war on Russia?

* *d* Why should the invasion of Belgium be regarded as of 'crucial importance in the course of the universal catastrophe' (lines 19–20)?

* *e* '[O]ne plan of campaign' (line 21). Explain the nature of the German military plan and the effect it had on German policy in the crisis leading to the outbreak of war.

* *f* Assess Germany's responsibility for the First World War.

6 Great Britain: 4 August 1914

The origins of the tension which developed between Great Britain and Germany at the end of the nineteenth century have been exhaustively described and analysed, and one thing at least can be said of them with little fear of contradiction. They cannot be attributed to simple political 5 or commercial rivalries. On both sides popular emotion ran faster and further than governmental policy. A careful calculation of state interests on both sides might have led, not perhaps to alliance, but at least to a *détente* comparable to that which British diplomats negotiated so successfully with France and Russia. The fundamental requirements for 10 such a *détente* would have been, on the one hand, British abstention from involvement in the Continental military balance which Germany saw as vital to her own security, and, on the other, German abstention from challenging the naval pre-eminence on which the British believed that their survival and that of the entire imperial system depended.

15 In Britain both popular and official opinion did in fact remain deeply hostile to the whole concept of any military involvement on the Continent; so hostile, indeed, that it was not evident to anyone until war had actually broken out whether a British Expeditionary Force would be committed there or not. In Germany on the other hand the new naval 20 policy reflected deep currents of popular emotion and powerful

economic interests which were concerned with a great deal more than national security. . . .

From 1909 the plans of the British Army, and after 1911 the plans of the Royal Navy, were based on the assumption that a German attack on
25 Belgium or France would be a *casus belli* for Britain; and that in that event the British Expeditionary Force would take its place on the left flank of the French armies. This assumption derived . . . from the political calculation that British security demanded that the balance of power in Europe should not be destroyed by the victory of the German Empire and
30 its allies over the forces of France and Russia; and from the military calculation that the presence of the British Expeditionary Force at what was assumed to be the decisive point would be just sufficient to balance the numerical superiority which the invading German armies might be expected to enjoy. Further, to get them to that point in time would
35 require careful preliminary preparations which would virtually eliminate all alternative options.

Asquith and his associates had not cared and possibly not dared to reveal either set of calculations to the British public, to Parliament, or even to all their colleagues in the Cabinet. When the moment came for
40 the plans of the military advisers to be put into effect they found themselves in an embarrassing predicament. From this embarrassment they were rescued, first by the German invasion of Belgium, which enabled them to justify British intervention on grounds not of power politics but of public law that commanded the support of the over-
45 whelming majority of their countrymen; and second, by the failure of the critics of the agreed military plans to come up with any equally well-prepared and closely reasoned alternatives.

Michael Howard, *The Continental Commitment: The Dilemma of British Defence Policy in the Era of the Two World Wars*, 1974, pp 31–2, 53–4

Questions

a Explain the following: (i) 'the new naval policy' (lines 19–20); (ii) '*casus belli*' (line 25).

b What is the difference between an alliance and a *détente*? How did the British *détentes* with France and Russia come about and what were the main points of the agreements? Did a basis in fact exist for the negotiation of a *détente* between Britain and Germany, 1900–14?

c Why should Asquith have been reluctant to reveal plans for British military involvement on the continent? Would a firm declaration of its intentions by the British government in 1914 have affected the European crisis?

* *d* What evidence is there that popular opinion did sway the governments in Britain and Germany in the years leading up to the First World War?

* *e* Why did Britain go to war with Germany in 1914?

Further Work

a What impressions have you formed from these extracts about the problems which faced the decision-makers of 1914 in handling any major crisis?

b Why, when so many crises were solved peacefully between 1871 and 1914, did that of 1914 end in war?

c Discuss how and why views have changed on the issue of Germany's responsibility for the outbreak of the First World War since 1918.